CW00684236

BEWARE OF LIVING TOO LONG!

...and other letters to my church family

by John Gillespie

edited by Sue Weller
foreword by Andy Paterson

DAY THREE EDITIONS
an imprint of Maritime Books

Beware Of Living Too Long!

First published 2010

First edition

Copyright © John Gillespie, 2010
The moral right of the author has been asserted

Published by Day Three Editions
an imprint of Maritime Books
Lodge Hill
Liskeard
PL14 4EL
UK

Printed in England by CPI Bookmarque, Croydon, CR0 4TD

ISBN 1 904459 50 1

This book is dedicated to
the life and witness of

Nathan Fisher
who joins the distinguished ranks of
those who lived well, though not long:

David Brainerd
Robert Murray M'Cheyne
Henry Martyn
Henry Scougal
Jim Elliot
Keith Green
John the Baptist
Our Lord Jesus Christ

CONTENTS

Foreword

Pastors can be passionate people... I don't mean that in the romantic sense but rather in the sense of those who go after something with all their heart. John is one of those men; there are no half-measures with him, whether that means swimming (which he does to 'championship' level), cycling or playing his guitars. And this same passion is very clearly seen within his natural and spiritual family. As a father and husband he leads and loves his wife and children with tender intensity. As a pastor and teacher he shepherds the flock under his care with unrelenting diligence and grace.

All these qualities are more than evident in this collection of pastoral letters. You can hear the laughter in his voice as he writes; you can see the tear splashed on the page as he weeps; you can sense the earnestness as he pleads and encourages. Here is a true pastor at work.

What makes John such a passionate man is that his heart has been captured by his passionate Saviour. As a result John has smelled the fires of hell and glimpsed the glories of heaven; he has been humbled by the cross and rescued by the crucified One. Here is a man who — more than any other I know — reflects the heart of Christ.

But not only is he a passionate man, he is also a wise and contemporary man. Sound Biblical scholarship is married to relevant application and driven into our hearts with insightful understanding. As a skilful swordsman he slices through our excuses and exposes the rottenness we would rather disguise.

Blessed indeed are the members of Grace Community Church to have such a loving pastor, and privileged are we to be able to listen in to this shepherdly care. Relish these letters — take them slowly and carefully — and experience them just as if they were written for you.

Andrew Paterson
Senior Pastor, Kensington Baptist Church, Bristol

INTRODUCTION

Grace Community Church sits high on a hill
overlooking the Cornish countryside.

Today it is a flourishing evangelical church with two
partner churches in nearby towns.

But its beginnings came as a result of much pain and
struggles for pastor John Gillespie, his family and
congregation. The story of Grace is told in another book
Not The Perfect Church.

Every week John Gillespie writes a letter to his church
family, to encourage, uplift, teach and sometimes warn.
This book contains a year of those letters.

We believe and hope you will find them relevant
and pertinent to your life.

Week 1

Satisfy us in the morning with Your unfailing love,
that we might sing for joy and be glad all of our days.
(Psalm 90:14)

Beware, Your Pastor Is Praying For You!

Dear Friends,

One of the great privileges that I have as your pastor is the privilege of praying for you. Samuel said to the people of Israel: 'Far be it from me that I should sin against the Lord by failing to pray for you' (1 Sam 12:23). I would be sinning against the Lord if I did not regularly pray for you.

Now, before you feel too comforted at the thought that your pastor is praying for you, I think it only fair that I clue you into just what I am praying! The verse at the top of my letter will point you in the directions of my prayers.

Psalm 90 is a great and majestic Psalm which magnifies the greatness of God and humbles proud man to his rightful place before Him. Having been duly humbled in the presence of a glorious God, the Psalmist (in this case Moses) lifts up his heart in prayer with the words:

'Satisfy us in the morning with Your unfailing love,
that we might sing for joy and be glad all of our days.'
(Psalm 90:14)

This is the prayer of a man who has been *rightly reduced* before a Holy God. Moses cried out, 'Lord, may *You* be that which satisfies my heart. May *You* be my true joy and the source of my gladness.'

Now, one of the problems we continually have as fallen (though redeemed) people, is the tendency to seek satisfaction everywhere but in the Lord. The world repeatedly becomes too attractive to us. Sometimes God has to wrench us away from the little gods we worship, and back to Himself for the good, and very survival of, our souls.

As your pastor, the essence of my prayer to you is this: 'Lord! Reduce them to Yourself! Get them to the place where they see that You and You alone are their hope, joy, peace and strength. Satisfy them, Lord, with Your unfailing love!'

10

Now, I realise that some of you are walking through the most severe trials right now. Truly I pray for the strength and comfort of the Lord Jesus to be yours. I in no way wish to appear to be indifferent to your pain. But I realise that tribulations often bring us into a new place with the Lord Jesus that is sweeter than the trial is bitter. Yet I still pray, 'Lord, be enough for them! Lord, use this suffering to reveal Your sufficiency.'

More than for those who are walking through difficult times, I have great concern for those of you for whom life is going swimmingly. Your soul is in greater danger when all seems well than when storms are battering you. I pray, 'Lord! Preserve them jealously for Yourself! Keep them from the twin idols of comfort and ease! *Reduce them to Yourself, Lord.*'

I do not pray for us to have easier lives. I pray for us to be consecrated to the cause of Christ. I do not pray for us to 'realise our potential' or 'improve our self image'. I pray for us to die to self. I do not pray for us to be happy with all that is surrounding us, but for us to feel what God feels... rejoicing when He rejoices and weeping when He weeps. I do not pray for us to get rich to the detriment of our souls. I pray for us to be captivated by the beauty of the Lord and the needs of the world, so that riches can no longer tempt us with their Siren-song. I often pray that the Lord will take us through the hard way, so that flesh will be exposed, and Christ will be seen as all-sufficient. I pray for our eyes to be on Heaven and for our treasure to be there. I pray that we will be ruined for the ordinary and alive to the extra-ordinary.

The bottom line of my prayer-life for you is that Jesus Christ will be seen and experienced as your Sufficient, Satisfying Saviour.

This is Holiness.

Now none of these prayers will feed your ego, increase your bank balance, guarantee health, reduce your wrinkles, or improve your romantic potential. They may, if our all wise and good God deems it necessary, do the exact opposite. But such pastoral praying will, if combined with a willingness on your part, help to reduce you to the place where Jesus is truly first in your heart and life. Then the joy of the Lord will be yours, and you will be the possessor of true wealth. You will be useful in the Master's service. You will become an even greater blessing to others. You will be dwelling, even now, in the outer precincts of Heaven.

Well, your pastor is praying for you... I hope you feel duly disturbed.

Yours,

John Gillespie.

Notes:~

Week 2

Thou desirest truth in the inward parts.
(Psalm 51:6)

Who Are You In The Secret Place?

Dear Church,

I was not certain this week whether to open my letter to you with a quote from the Bible or from Groucho Marx. No, I have not begun to backslide, nor have I somehow lost my bearings. But sometimes inspiration can come from the strangest of sources. I guess I will put both quotes before you... and trust that you will be able to 'spot the difference.'

'These are my principles, and if you don't like them...
well, I have others.'
G Marx

'Behold [I like that word!] Thou desirest truth in the inward parts.'
King David

I trust you can look beyond the comedy of Groucho's quip to discern its tragic reflection of our ages in each of our lives.

After an initial chuckle at Groucho's statement, I began to ponder the fact that it actually reveals much of the spirit of our generation. Where are men and women who are governed by fixed internal *principles* as opposed to mere passing *interests*? We rarely find people of *substance* today, for we live in an age of *shadows*. We live in a world that plays to please the crowd, but ignores the God before whom we all must give an account. As such we are becoming increasingly shallow as a culture. We tell ourselves that the private lives of our leaders (and therefore of ourselves) is of little consequence, but God thinks otherwise.

An acquaintance of Lloyd-George said of him that when he was all alone *there was no one there*. Consider the tragedy of that statement. He had become a man of public image, not of private substance. He lived for the crowd.

King David, for all of his flaws, at least understood that God is after *character*, not just *image*. It is what a man is in the secret place, where no one sees, that really counts. The first quote betrays a lack of character, a flaw in the inner man, that will render him spineless. At least David's cry reveals a yearning for inner *substance*, which will render him bold before men.

God is concerned with our character. He is concerned that we be on the *inside* what the public sees on the *outside*. One's conduct in *private* should not be essentially different from one's conduct in *public*. Who we are on Saturday night is as important as who we are on Sunday morning. *What* we do must line up with *Who* we are. But as we no longer expect such integrity of our leaders, we excuse the lack of it in ourselves. David rebukes and instructs our age: 'You desire truth in the inner place.'

Now this is all very challenging. But our God is about Truth. He is not a spin doctor. There is no place in God that is not genuine. He is on the outside what He is in the inside. He is not just a God of appearance, but of substance. He is who He says He is and is what He appears to be. *His* principles are fixed and *His* character is true. What He is in the 'privacy' of His triune being, He is in *His* public appearances. And *we* need to take our cues from the God of the Bible and not from the characters in Hollywood, or Westminster, or The White House.

I think I can go so far as to say that God is more concerned with our character than with our gifts. I am sure that I can go so far as to say that *we* should be too; Godliness of heart and life should be our greatest of concerns. If we work on the inner life, the outer life will take care of itself. If we yearn for *substance* and leave the *shadows*, we will find ourselves being bold before men and honoured before God.

Let's strive for Godliness way down deep. What God wants first is for us to be a people of integrity... substance... Godly character... private virtue. If we are diligent at that level, the Lord will be sure to be with us.

Image: how we *appear* before men.

Character: what God *sees* in us.

Yours,

John Gillespie.

Notes:~

Week 3

I have been crucified with Christ and I no longer live,
but Christ lives in me.
The life I live in the body, I live by faith in the Son of God,
who loved me and gave Himself for me.
(Galatians 2:20)

Ruined For The Ordinary

Dear Church Family,

It is a joy to write to you on the eve of our missions weekend:
The Call.

I want to encourage all of us to make every effort to be present
whenever possible at these important meetings, that we may
hear, together, from the Lord concerning His heart for the Glory of
His Son and the joy of all peoples.

In setting the stage for the weekend, I want to challenge us with
the amazing life testimony of a new found hero of mine, William
Borden. William was born in Chicago in 1887. He was born into a
very wealthy family, and was a millionaire from childhood. He was
saved through the preaching of the famous evangelist, Billy
Sunday. At the age of sixteen, William's father sent him on a
world cruise. He saw the needs of the world and, as a young
Christian man, he would never be the same. He was ruined for the
ordinary!

He went to university at Yale, and then on to Princeton. He led
the way for Christ among the students, and spiritual awakening
tended to happen wherever this consecrated young man was
found. But his heart was on a mission! Soon the newspapers
carried the headline: 'Young Millionaire Gives Away Fortune for
the Mission Field.' Considered a fool by many, Borden gave his
fortune away and set sail for China, being called to a certain
Muslim tribe.

He stopped in Cairo, determined to learn Arabic for the sake of
his outreach to Muslims. While there, he contracted meningitis
and died at the age of twenty-five. When the news of his death
reached America the story of his life and devotion to Christ
generated a fresh wave of interest in sacrificial service amongst
the Christians of his generation. A life that, to onlookers, seemed
to be a waste was, in the providential hands of God, supremely

used. He is buried in the American Cemetery in Cairo. Upon his tombstone are inscribed the words: 'Apart from Jesus Christ, there is no explanation for such a life.'

William Borden's life stood in stark contrast to the values of his generation, and his legacy of giving all for Christ stands as a stern rebuke to the self-centred values of our day. He heard the call of Jesus Christ to find his life by losing it, and followed. The lukewarm, the culturally-conformed, the fair-weather follower and the prosperity preacher have no answer for such a life.

In the back of his Bible it was found that he had written six words...

No Reserves
No Retreat
No Regrets

Take some time and meditate upon those words. Measure your life by them. Be tough on yourself. Ask yourself: 'What will be written on *my* tombstone?' Hold your life up to the light of Eternity, and dare to measure it by the values of Heaven.

Beloved, this is no time to hold back. This is *our time to go forward*. God is calling us to what the world will see as radical, but what the Kingdom sees as normal; joyful, crucified following of Jesus Christ. I believe that God can do the unimaginable through a crucified, consecrated church!

Let's expect God to work in our hearts and lives this weekend. Let's come willing to be challenged. How about actually *asking* the lord to take us, together, into new areas of sacrifice and joyous service. That is what I am asking of the Lord.

May we, together, be 'Ruined for the Ordinary.'

Yours,

John Gillespie.

Notes:~

Week 4

He makes His…servants flames of fires.
(Hebrews 1:7)

'Let Me Not Sink To Be A Clod'

Dear Brothers and Sisters,

We all have much to rejoice about in the wake of 'The Call'.

I am sure that most of us have taken time to reflect upon the weekend.

As I reflect upon our time together, a few very precious things stand out. First of all, it was just good to be together, as a church family, and as a family of churches. Our fellowship together was wonderful. Next, I was amazed at just how much ministry is flowing from us! The Lord truly is at work in our midst, calling us, empowering us, and releasing us into so many different forms of service. Moreover, I know we only saw the tip of the iceberg as far as ministries are concerned. We are a church made up of 'unsung heroes'… just ordinary followers of the Lord Jesus who are 'getting on with it' in our various spheres of influence. I know that a church without 'superstars' blesses the Lord and is also a very powerful weapon in His hands. He alone deserves all the credit for the abundance of blessing flowing from this church.

Of course, I was blessed and encouraged by the ministry from God's Word to us.

Let's just recall the three main points shared from the pulpit:
1. *What* is Mission?
   'The purposeful crossing of boundaries of unbelief with the Gospel.' We can *all* be doing this in no end of ways!

2. *Why* Mission?
   Can you remember all the 'C's' we talked about? The Calling; Compassion; Comprehensive plan; Covenant; Celebration, among others.

3. *How* Mission?
   Beginning where we are, perhaps doing what we don't want to do, with people we don't want to be with, in a place we don't want to be… *but God can use us!*

What is important now is that we take what we have learned, been blessed by, been convicted of, *and act upon it*. Do not allow yourself to waste God's Word to you and work in you. If the Lord spoke to you in any way, ask Him for grace to act accordingly. *Get on with it.*

I was reconvinced of the fact that we are living in Gospel days. This is not the time for us to move into our evangelical ghetto and wait for the end to come. These days are days for the Gospel to be declared. Society has run out of answers and options. The answer for our world is the Lord Jesus Christ. I am more convinced of this now than I have ever been. I want to warn us off a way of thinking that will kill evangelism and stop us dead in our tracks. If we allow a mentality to creep in that suggests that God is not able to empower us to meet the needs of our day, then we have had it. If we forget that we are called to be soldiers, and not tourists, we will never persevere. If we ignore the fact that we are in a spiritual battle for the very souls of our generation, then we will shun the sacrifices that the Gospel is going to demand of us as we press forward. God is able, but we must be willing. We dare not think that God is in recession! Ask God for more grace. Ask Him to make us soldiers. Ask Him to convict you of the values of Heaven and the needs of the world.

I leave you with a powerful poem by Amy Carmichael:

From prayer that asks that I may be
Sheltered from winds that beat on Thee,
From fearing when I should aspire,
From faltering when I should climb higher,
From silken self, O Captain, free
Thy soldier who would follow Thee.
From subtle love of softening things,
From easy choices, weakenings,
(Not thus are spirits fortified,
Not this way went the Crucified),
From all that dims Thy Calvary
O Lamb of God, deliver me.

Give me the love that leads the way,
The faith that nothing can dismay,
The hope no disappointments tire,
The passion that will burn like fire;
Let me not sink to be a clod;
Make me Thy fuel, Flame of God.

Please make that poem your prayer.

Yours,

John Gillespie.

Notes:~

Week 5

...pursue righteousness, godliness, faith, love, endurance,
and gentleness. Fight the good fight of the faith.
(1 Timothy 6:11-12)

God Doesn't Do Downloads

Dear Brothers and Sisters in Christ,

I was struck this week by a quote by my friend and former Bible
Week* speaker Chris Short:

> 'God doesn't do downloads.'

Think with me about this for a minute. What is a 'download'? Those
of us with computers have become used to them. (Those of you not
familiar with computers please bear with me for a few minutes.)
When you want something new on your computer, some new bit of
information, or music, or some new capacity of ability, you simply
push a few certain buttons, wait a few minutes, and... there it
appears on your computer, 'downloaded' and ready for you to use
and enjoy. The whole process is comparatively effortless and
trouble-free!

We are becoming used to expecting a 'download' lifestyle. We want
the path of least resistance. We want something for nothing. We
want discipleship without cost and Heaven without sweat.

We want a God who 'downloads'...

> 'God! Download me some joy.'
> 'God! Download me some peace.'
> 'I want to know you more... download spiritual intimacy with You!'
> 'A better marriage!' 'Happiness!'

> 'God! Download for me...
> purpose...
> obedient kids...
> victory over sin...
> weight loss...
> a clean house...'

Yes, God moves upon us by His wonderful grace, answers prayer, and
blesses us more than ever we deserve. But He makes it clear in His
word that He is not Lord of the instant! He is not the download God.

His Word is full of commands for Christians... little words with big meanings such as:

> 'Do not *let* sin reign in you'
> 'Put *off* the old self'
> 'Put *on* the new self'

> *'Study'*
> *'Do your best'*
> *'Make every effort'*
> *'Wait'*
> *'Follow'*
> *'Pursue'*
> *'Fight'*

These are not 'download' words! They *require* something of us. *Yes*, we are saved and kept and sanctified by grace. But grace *enables*, it does not *excuse*. It *empowers the weak*, it does not *lift the lazy*. These words go against the grain of a download culture. To expect God to magically impart a deep, meaningful, purposeful knowledge of Himself to you while you watch TV and ignore His Word is... frankly... foolishness. To expect God to download victory over Satan and sin while one sits passively is... purely... presumption.

God is not going to:

> Clean your desk for you...

> Get fit for you...

> Download Truth for you...

> Witness to your neighbour for you...

> Love your wife or husband for you...

What God *will do* is grant a super abundance of Grace that we might look to Him, be strengthened by Him, and do what we may not 'feel' like doing, or downright cannot do at all without His power being made perfect in our weakness...

> The Lord will enable us to serve joyfully in our families and communities... but we need to *pray and ask* Him for strength... and then *do the work*.

The Lord will impart a true and life-changing knowledge of Himself to us... but we need to *turn off the TV* and *open our Bibles.*

Men, the Lord will enable you to love the wife of your youth... but you need to *go buy her flowers* (even when you don't feel like it) and *stop looking at other women.*

Ladies, God will give you a content heart, but you will need to get into the Word and out of the world.

The Lord will grant us grace for giving, but we need to *die to self* and get our *priorities lined up with the values of His Kingdom.*

Chris Short is right... God doesn't do downloads!

But, since He does give grace...

...You are as Holy as you want to be.

So... Let's get on with it.

Yours,

John Gillespie.
(*See *For More Information* at the end of the book)

Notes:~

Week 6

*Now to Him who is able to do immeasurably more
than all we ask or imagine,
according to His power that is within us, to
Him be glory in the church
and in Christ Jesus throughout all generations,
for ever and ever! Amen.
(Ephesians 3:20,21)*

Meditations On Putting My Dog Down
And Wanting My Sick Mother To Live

Dear Family in Christ,

The following pastoral letter is a good bit longer than most, and deals with a sensitive matter. I trust you will receive it with a generous spirit.

As many will know, my family and I said goodbye this week to our long-time faithful dog and friend Duke. Many of you will understand that the word 'pet' is insufficient to describe the relationship which can develop between a good dog and his master. Duke will be warmly remembered, not only by me and my family, but by many of you who knew and loved him. We together are most thankful for his sixteen years of life.

As a family, we decided together that it was time to have Duke 'put down'. In reaching this decision, I had to do some Biblical thinking, basically grappling with the question:

*What gives me the right to decide that it is time for an animal,
which God created, to die?*

In the process, another question cast a shadow over me, and refused to let me ignore it:

*How can you be merciful in not wanting your dog to suffer, and
then be willing to have your own mother, a person, suffer, refusing
her a 'dignified death?'*

In other words, why is it right to 'put a dog down', and wrong to perform euthanasia? Should people be allowed to suffer pain and distress where we would, in mercy, not allow an animal to suffer?

These two questions are joined at the hip, and it is really important that Christians be able to give a clear answer to both. We regularly hear in the news of families flying overseas to give their loved ones the opportunity to end their pain-filled lives in ways not dissimilar to the way in which a vet ended my dear dog's life. There is increasing pressure upon our society to embrace the 'merciful' killing of the aged and infirmed, and to view those who oppose such actions as lacking compassion.

The first question is very easy to answer from a Biblical standpoint. At Creation God ordained that man should have dominion over animals:

> *Then God said: 'Let us make man in our image...and let them rule*
> *over the fish of the sea and the birds of the air,*
> *over the livestock, over all the earth, and over all the creatures*
> *that move along the ground.' (Genesis 1:26)*

This Creation Ordinance means that God has delegated His rule over creatures to mankind. As God's vice-regents, we are finally accountable to God for the well-being of every creature on earth. But we also have sovereignty over them. A good master is responsible for his animal's life. This implies a delegated authority to decide when it is time for his animal's life to end. Never forgetting his accountability to God, the Man, made in God's Image, has dominion over the animal. It is as simple and as profound as that. When I decided that Duke was beginning to suffer in a way that would be detrimental to his overall well-being, and beyond my *finite* ability to cope (God's ability to cope is *infinite*), then, with a thankful and reverent eye toward *my* Lord, *I* presided over *his* death.

No-one has suggested that my family and I have been anything but prudent and merciful.

Why, then, can I not suggest the same course of action for my long-term ill, 'invalid' (horrible word!), pain-filled mother? Why do I, along with my family, applaud the efforts of the doctors to give her every chance to live another day, as we wait for her life to end naturally? Why have some of you chosen palliative care for a pain-racked relative rather than succumb to the mounting pressure to 'mercifully end their life'?

I want to give four reasons why it is wrong to perform euthanasia, and not unmerciful to patiently endure with a suffering human who himself is patiently enduring as they await their own death. The following is by no means an exhaustive treatment of the subject, and I am well aware that there are many 'what ifs' that arise in situations where tragic suffering is found.

1) While God has bestowed upon us a delegated sovereignty over the animal kingdom, He has retained sole sovereignty over those made in His Image. Euthanasia is an act of insubordination on our part. The Bible makes it plain that 'our times are in *His* hands' (Psalm 31:15), and that *God* has 'ordained our days' (Psalm 139:16). To stretch mercy for animals which ends in 'putting them down' to a justification for the 'mercy killing' of suffering humans is to confuse categories within the basic order of Creation and to usurp our place as creatures under the Sovereign Lordship of God.

2) Suffering has a redemptive purpose for humans which it can never have in animals. Animals have not been created in God's Image. They were not the immediate objects of Christ's Atonement. They are not rebels in need of salvation. The Bible never speaks of them being justified by grace through faith, and they cannot grow in holiness. But for people, it is a different matter. God wills our sanctification, our transformation, our growth in holiness. As such, it is a plain fact both of Scripture and experience that suffering often does a work in the soul of the sufferer that pleasure cannot. Peter boldly writes:

'Therefore, since Christ suffered in His body, arm yourselves also with the same attitude, because he who has suffered in his body is done with sin. As a result, he does not live the rest of his earthly life for evil human desires but rather for the will of God.
(1 Peter 4:1,2)

Euthanasia can cut off the sanctifying work of God in the child of God before God would have it cut off. It is not hard to imagine that it could even prevent one coming to Christ by cutting their life short before conversion.

3) Suffering Christians can be powerfully used of God as Gospel witnesses and workers. David Brainard, Amy Carmichael, Joni Ericson-Tada... the list goes on and on. There are many in our own fellowships who bear powerful witness to the grace of God through their pain and suffering. The apostle Paul reminded the Galatians:

'As you know it was because of an illness that I first preached the Gospel to you.' (Galatians 4:13)

I know of very ill saints, suffering long-term illnesses, leading others, including sick and dying unbelievers in hospital, to Christ.

Jesus Christ uses saints, often in weakness and infirmity, to manifest His manifold mercies.

Grace is also remarkably manifested through those who care for the infirm. Pain affords a remarkable opportunity for the nature of God to be manifested in the hearts and lives of those who love and support those who suffer. What an opportunity suffering affords to prove that indeed he *does* 'give strength to the weary' and 'increase the power of the weak'.

4) Because we are a sinful and fallen race, we can get it wrong with euthanasia. Conceivably, I got it wrong with my dear dog. Perhaps he would have rallied next week and gone on for a year or two. But where people are concerned, we cannot afford ourselves the luxury of being right 'most of the time'.

I personally have been pastorally present in tragic cases where there has been no glimmer of hope... only to see people defy all odds and confound all expectations and recover. Moreover, we fallen ones cannot be trusted with the power of life and death over the weak... It is too open to abuse in our hands, and therefore best left in God's. It is by no means beyond conception that any of us could be tempted to 'bump off Granny' because we could really use her flat. Sorry if that offends, but I fear it is too true.

Authority over Duke was delegated to me by the Sovereign Lord. I exercised it in determining that it was time for his days to end. Authority, in matters of life and death, over my mother, and every human being, belongs to God alone. It is our place to humbly wait, worship, alleviate, and care for the weakest in our midst. May God have mercy upon us as a culture as we are increasingly challenging where He has placed us in His Created Order.

Well, I warned you of a long and sensitive letter. I trust we see more clearly the importance of understanding what it means to have dominion on the one hand, and to be under Christ's Lordship on the other, and how vital it is that we understand the difference.

May the Lord lead us to live in these days as wise and effective disciples.

Yours,

but only for His Glory,

John Gillespie.

Notes:~

Week 7

For He performeth the thing that is appointed for me;
and many such things are with Him. (Job 23:14)

Disappointment ~ His Appointment

Dear Brothers and Sisters,

As we are on the eve of Bible Week the Lord has brought a poem
to mind that has been with me for many years. I have a feeling it
is going to apply to many of you.

Disappointment is a close cousin of brokenness... and they are
often found in company together.

I want to encourage you to meditate on the words below by Edith
Lillian Young. Prayerfully use them to help you prepare for the
Lord to minister to and through you this week. If you are going
through a time of disappointment, or know someone who is, may
the Biblical wisdom revealed in this masterful poem speak a word
of healing and wholeness to you.

Jesus Christ loves you.

Yours,

John Gillespie.

Disappointment — His Appointment

'Disappointment — His Appointment'
Change one letter, then I see
That the thwarting of my purpose
Is God's better choice for me.
His appointment must be blessing,
Tho' it may come in disguise,
For the end from the beginning
Open to His wisdom lies.

'Disappointment — His Appointment'
Whose? The Lord, who loves me best,
Understands and knows me fully,
Who my faith and love would test;
For, like loving earthly parent,
He rejoices when He knows
That His child accepts, UNQUESTIONED,
All that from His wisdom flows.

'Disappointment — His Appointment'
'No good thing will He withhold'
From denials oft we gather
Treasures of His love untold,
Well He knows each broken purpose
Leads to fuller, deeper trust,
And the end of all His dealings
Proves our God is wise and just.

'Disappointment — His Appointment'
Lord, I take it, then, as such.
Like the clay in hands of potter,
Yielding wholly to Thy touch.
All my life's plan in Thy moulding,
Not one single choice be mine;
Let me answer, unrepining —
'Father, not my will, but Thine.'

Edith Lillian Young

Notes:~

29

Week 8

Run in such a way as to get the prize.
(1 Corinthians 9:24)

See You On The Podium

Dear Church Family,

I don't know about you, but I love the Olympics. My whole family loves the Games. Every four years we get a TV licence and find ourselves up early, and staying up late, just to watch. No, more than just to watch... we really get *into it*. (I even find myself daydreaming that *I* am the great competitor, the champion... except in Beach Volleyball!)

I think I have broken the code on just *what it is* about the Games that I find so compelling. I am certain that it is the thrill, the inspiration, of watching men and women *give their best* at something they have *given themselves to*. Do we realise just what it takes to rise to the top in a sport, or for that matter in art, or in *any* endeavour? Just think about the early mornings out of bed, pounding the pavement in the cold rain. Imagine the lonely nights staying in when friends are out 'living it up'. Consider the denial of one's self, the saying 'no' to the impulses for immediate gratification with food or drink, pleasure or play, in the hope of a future reward. Ponder the lonely hours of practice with no crowds to cheer one on, when muscles ache and bones are weary... all in the hope of being the very best that you can be.

When we see a Paula Radcliffe, a Michael Phelps or a Nicola Cooke standing on the winners' podium bathing in the glory of victory, what we are seeing is the *fruit* borne of the loneliness of commitment. When you hear Jonathan Delbridge [one of our church musicians] with seeming effortless ease playing his instrument to the glory of God, what you are hearing is the joyous payoff of thousands of weary hours of lonely practice.

Such excellence is a rare jewel in a culture that makes a hero of donut-eating Homer Simpson. How many of us will flop on the couch tonight and stare at the TV, munching away on a bag of crisps, quietly desperate at just what we have become, when deep down inside we *know we were purposed for so much more*.

'I could have done that,' we will boast to our fellow couchmates... but the fact is that *we never paid the price required for the prize*.

30

Now, I have never really been a paid up member of the Couch Club. I have always been a pretty determined person. Nevertheless, I am having to come to terms with the possibility...
probability...
FACT...
... that I am not going to win Olympic Gold.

But! There is another prize... a BIGGER prize that I am still in the running for. And so are you.

Take a few minutes to stare at these words of the Apostle. Let the weight of them impact you.

Do you not know that in a race all the runners run,
but only one gets the prize?
Run in such a way as to get the prize.
(1 Corinthians 9:24)

I press on toward the goal to win the prize for which
God has called me heavenward in Christ Jesus.
(Philippians 3:14)

Everyone who competes in the games goes into strict training.
They do it to get a crown that will not last;
but we do it to get a crown that will last forever.
Therefore I do not run like a man running aimlessly;
I do not fight like a man beating the air.
(1 Corinthians 9:25, 26)

Okay, I give you that we are saved and kept by grace and grace alone. There is *nothing* that we can add to the finished saving work of Jesus Christ. But that does not mean that we are meant to be passive observers as opposed to active participants in the greatest contest in all the world. We are called to live for Christ in a world that crucified Him. The Apostle views the Christian life as a race to be run with a prize to be won: the prize of living a Christ-glorifying life; the prize of seeing Him honoured in and among His People and among the nations of the world; the prize of knowing that our lives are being lived for a purpose greater than ourselves and more lasting than our brief years on earth.

So, how about a bit of grit and determination? How about some Olympian-like sacrifice and passion from us? What about weighing up our lives in the light of Eternity? Is it not about time for some tough decisions? Are you a 'Couch Christian'? That just won't cut it in these days of Gospel opportunity. Imagine that great day when all human glory is faded, when the medals and prizes of Time have tarnished before the reality of Eternity. Imagine an unfading Crown of Life being yours, but more; imagine the Lord Jesus, *your* Lord Jesus, being glorified among a redeemed creation. Consider knowing that *your grace-empowered life* was lived *at full stretch* for that very glory of Christ, that you got up off your sofa, turned off your TV, and really *lived* for Him.

Whatever sacrifices you made will pale into insignificance on that great day.

See you in the pool... then one day on the podium!

Yours,

John Gillespie.

Notes:~

*'But we all, with open face beholding as in a glass the glory of the
Lord, are changed into the same image from glory to glory,
even as by the Spirit of the Lord.'*
(2 Corinthians 3:18)

Gaze At The Lord

Dear Church,

I love the Bible. I love the Bible's perspective on reality. The Bible
is a book about God's Son, Jesus, and it has the power to
change lives.

The Bible flips over our view of things and, given that we were
seeing and living upside down, now enables us to see things right
side up. For instance, take a few moments to think on the verse
found at the top of this page. Do you get what it is saying? It is
saying something that the world will never say, but something that
Christians need to know and put great stock in. In a nutshell, the
verse says *seeing is becoming*. Do you see that? The world says
'seeing is believing', but God says 'seeing is *becoming*'. That is, as
we take long, unhurried, beholding looks at Jesus, we are
continually and increasingly changed into His likeness. We become
like Him as we look at Him.

But here is a good, and obvious, question: how can we look at One
whom we cannot see? Where do we go to gaze? Is it something only
the fortunate few can do? Does gazing upon Christ demand a rare
and fertile imagination, or a monastic mysticism? Can ordinary
Christians like us do this?

Let me take you back to the 15th century, to Holland, and to a
Christian thinker named Desidirius Erasmus. He loved the Bible and
was concerned to get the best translation possible into circulation.
He gave his generation a new translation of the New Testament. Let
me give you my very favourite quote of his:

'The Bible will give Christ to you in an intimacy so close
that He would be less visible to you if He stood before your eyes.'
(Erasmus)

Now, not only do I believe that Erasmus was right, I have built my
entire Christian experience and my whole preaching ministry
around this wonderful, vital truth. I can't physically see Jesus...

yet. But I have His Bible. I can see Jesus very clearly in the Bible. I do not believe that the Bible is a dead book, but a living one. *I actually believe that the Bible gives me a clearer understanding of the Lord Jesus than the disciples had when He was before their eyes.* I can 'gaze' at the Lord in the Bible. I can ask the Holy Spirit to illuminate the Word to me and to help me see Jesus Christ. Just like the two disciples on the Emmaus Road, *my* heart can burn within *me* as I see Him in the Book of books.

I want you to glory in this truth with me. We *can* see the Lord with a certainty. We can behold Him and in so doing, we can be changed into His likeness. I have to tell you in all honesty, and with a good bit of humility, that if you *don't* believe this truth about the Bible, you probably won't be very satisfied with what I have to offer as a pastor and as a preacher. Christ is offered today through the Scriptures. This is a sure offering, a clear offering, a life-changing offering, a world-changing offering.

Let me give you a case and point: in this church we will be beginning a sermon series soon on the Book of Revelation. It is my aim and hope that we will see Christ in Revelation, because *He* is what the book is *about*. Just notice with me what God said to John about the revelation that he was about to receive:

> 'The voice said, "Write in a **book** what you **see**.
> Then send it to the... churches."'
> (Revelation 1:11)

Get this: John gets the vision, we get the book. "Write in a *book* what you *see*, then send it to the churches." Now we need to believe that getting the *book* is as good as getting the *vision*. If we don't believe this, we will forever be feeling short-changed and second-rate. Many people would rather have the vision than the book, but the book is sure and true, and in it we see Christ as certainly as the ancient John in his vision on Patmos.

I want to challenge you to seek Jesus Christ afresh and for yourself in the Bible. Don't settle for less than a heart-felt encounter with the Living Christ through the Spirit-illuminated pages of Scripture. *Gaze upon Christ in the Book and in so doing you will become increasingly like Him.* Too many Christians leave their Bibles to collect dust and then wonder why they have no dynamic spiritual life. We neglect God's Word and then ask Him for intimacy. We won't get it.

To sing:

> 'Open the eyes of my heart Lord, I want to see you,'

but then ignore our Bibles is to ask God for something that is not on offer; an experience of Christ divorced from the Scriptures.

If you want intimacy with the real Christ, not one that you conjure up in your imagination, open your Bible, raise your heart to Heaven asking the Holy Spirit to shine on the sacred page, and you will see Jesus Christ, the Lord of Eternity, and the Saviour of sinners. Believe me. Millions through the ages have beheld their Saviour while still treading on this lonely planet. They have had genuine Spirit-filled encounters with Christ with their Bibles open and their hearts hungry, and in so doing have been increasingly changed to become like Him.

Erasmus is right.

We are as spiritually rich as we want to be.

Yours,

John Gillespie.

Notes:~

Week 10

These that have turned the world upside down.
(Acts 17:6)

Why We Call Our Dogs Caesar And Our Sons Paul*

Dear Church,

In his prophetic book *How Should We Then Live?* Francis Schaeffer looks back at the Roman Empire in its decline and draws vital applications for us in our day. Drawing from an eighteenth century volume by Edward Gibbons *The Decline and Fall of the Roman Empire*, Schaeffer highlights the five key traits of the Roman Empire as it reached its end. They make for sobering reading:

1. A mounting love of show and luxury (affluence)
2. A widening gap between the very rich and the very poor
3. An obsession with sex
4. Freakishness in the Arts masquerading as originality and creativity
5. An increased desire to live off the State

Schaeffer then states the all too obvious: 'It all sounds so familiar... we are back in Rome.'

Now, brothers and sisters, I have no desire to be a prophet of doom. I want to be a preacher of Good News. Likewise, I long for us to be a people saturated in the Joy that the Lord alone can give to otherwise ruined sinners. But, we do need to understand our times! If we are to be effective in our generation, then it is imperative that we understand the nature of our society.

It does not take a prophet to look at those five traits highlighted by Gibbons and see that indeed we today have gone full circle... right back to Rome. I could take time to comment on each one and to demonstrate the contemporary relevance of each in turn... but there is no need to. You can do that for yourselves. What is of vital importance is that we ask the question that Schaeffer asks in the title of his book: in light of the times in which we are living, '*how should we then live?*'

I believe that we are living through the rapid decline of the West. We were once a culture largely shaped by Christian values. Our sense of right and wrong, our democratic freedoms, our compassionate institutions, our valuing of life and the dignity of the individual, all of which we take so much for granted, all grew in a soil cultivated by the Gospel. The great freedoms that are now considered to be rights, are actually rare gifts that few societies in history have been given to enjoy. The freedom of self-determination, the ownership of property, and the fair accumulation of wealth, are preciously rare privileges which we have been granted in trust for our safe-keeping. Charitable institutions, hospitals and schools were developed best in the countries where men and women had their values shaped by Christ and His Gospel. Even the development of sport and fair play was a product of a culture in which individuals had their minds and values shaped by a Bible that taught that there was a God of order and fairness behind all human activities.

For all of the faults in Western culture (and there are many), never before in history have so many people enjoyed so much freedom, and at the same time risen to such levels of social compassion and concern...

And it is all a product of the Gospel being preached and Christians being Salt and Light in their society.

But! We are now living in an age which *demands* all of the benefits, but rejects the moral responsibility without which the benefits *cannot* be sustained. We want personal peace and prosperity without the moral compass to guide us. The freedoms we have enjoyed and the blessings they have brought to so many have been founded upon *the ability of individuals to govern themselves because they knew themselves to be personally accountable to God Himself.* As we reject Christ's Lordship over us but like spoiled children insist still upon all the 'goodies' that can come only through Christ and His Gospel, we actually render ourselves, as individuals and as a culture, unfit for the freedoms we now take for granted.

So, how do we, as believers, live in today's world? Exactly as Christians did in the early Church. Our ancient brothers and sisters put Christ ahead of comfort, and principles ahead of personal peace and prosperity. They too were living in a culture without a compass. The sun was setting upon a decadent Rome that had grown rich and soft at the expense of virtue. Yet these ancient Christians boldly followed Christ, even to their deaths. The Gospel outlived their culture, even as that culture did all it could to stamp it out. It is no accident that we today call our *dogs* Caesar and our *sons* Paul!

These are days of opportunity for us. Our culture will see either 1: Revival or 2: Ruin. I pray it is the first but I aim, by grace, to live for Christ no matter what. *If* believers live with an eye on Heaven, they will make an impact for Christ here below, God may have mercy on our land and restore something of a Christian mind to our generation, or perhaps to the next one. *If* we get on with evangelism and passionate concern for our neighbours, there may yet be a turning back to the Lord, even as there was 250 years ago during the Methodist Revival. What we dare not do is draw the curtains, turn on the TV, sink down in our sofas and let the world go by, as long as we are personally comfortable.

That is simply not a Christian option.

These are Gospel Days! Let's live for Christ *today*!

Grace and Peace,

John Gillespie.

('And pray for me too. Ask God to give me the right words so I can boldly explain God's mysterious plan that the Good News is for Jews and Gentiles alike.' Ephesians 6:19)

*Title credit to F F Bruce

Notes:~

*I press on toward the goal to win the price for which
God has called me heavenward in Christ Jesus.
(Philippians 3:14)*

Beware Of Living Too Long!

Dear Brothers and Sisters,

In 1982 I bought a book called *The Christian in Complete Armour*. It
was written in about 1650 by a faithful pastor named William
Gurnall. I still have not finished it! The book is an exposition of
Ephesians 6:10-18, Paul's famous passage on the 'armour of God',
which all true soldiers are urged to put on that we may fight the
fight of faith valiantly and successfully. While it focuses on only
eight Bible verses, the book is well over a thousand pages long!
In the early pages of the book, Gurnall gives five resolutions that a
Christian must have if he is to 'make it' through this earthly
sojourn. These have been a great comfort to me over the years and
have served to shape my mind in the midst of battle. I want to
share them with you today, in the hope that these five resolutions
will become a part of your life, even as they have of mine.

How to Keep on Your Way to Heaven:
Five Resolutions for the Battling Believer

1. Wage an irreconcilable war against your own heart sins. Many
of us wage such a war against the *visible* sins of those around us.
But the problems arise from our *own* hearts. Some sins are
comparatively easy to deal, and dispense, with. Others may take
years of battle... perhaps even a lifetime. The key is to declare and
wage a holy war against them. Repentance and coming to the cross
in faith and brokenness is our greatest weapon against the
accusation of our enemy. Holiness does not imply the absence of sin
so much as a resolution to wage war against sin.

2. Determine not to follow the fashions of this world. We are not
called to be cool, but holy! The Bible warns us to 'love not the
world'... not meaning the beautiful sunset and flowers and birds,
but the godless, wicked ways of our rebellious race. We are not to
take our values from this world and seek to 'fit in'. We are called
to swim upstream, not float downstream. Many lose Heaven
because they are ashamed to be thought foolish for following
Christ. It takes holy resolve to go one way when the crowd is going
another, but such must be the decision of a follower of Christ.

3. Keep going when others give up! As tough as it may sound, some who are battling with us today, seemingly living for Christ right alongside us, may give up, and change sides. The saddest words in the Bible may be found in Paul's last letter to Timothy: 'Demas, having loved this world, has turned back.' You must resolve now that Christ will be your best friend, and your most treasured companion. *Others will let you down.* It is a great discouragement when others faint and give up! Ask the Lord for strength to resolve to follow when others make a shipwreck of their faith.

4. Trust in God when you can't find Him. Sometimes God seems to be so very real... we feel as though we could reach out and touch Him. Sometimes God seems to withdraw from us. Sometimes He does not seem to be answering when we call. God is sovereign in all His ways and good in all that He does. We need to settle that right now. He may seemingly withdraw, for His own wise reasons, often unknown to us, and at such times we need to *trust in Him when we cannot find Him.* Such seasons bear their own special fruit, and then they pass, but we need to resolve now to trust Him through the foggy days as well as the sunny.

5. Make it your goal that your service for Christ and your days on earth shall finish together. Some people live too long! They seem to outlive their zeal for Christ and their love for Him! Make it your goal that you will not retire from following and serving. Perhaps your health will leave you and you will not have your natural strength. But that will not mean that your service for Christ need end! He will always have something of eternal worth for you to do. If your goal is to retire and live the easy life, you may end up with a cold, worldly heart. You may retire from secular employment, that is fine, but always make it your goal to serve Christ while you have breath.

Well, such was Gurnall's good advice. It has served me well since 1982, and continues to do so to this day. Take some time to meditate upon it. Find scriptures to buttress each resolution. Pray them into your life. Make sure that you are earnest about pressing on to Heaven. Yes, God is faithful, and His grace is sure, but our calling is not to laziness, but to vigilance.

May the Lord cause His grace to abound in you as you trust in Him and follow after Him.

'We want each of you to show this same diligence to the very end, in order to make your hope sure.
We do not want you to become lazy, but to imitate those who through faith and patience inherit what has been promised.'
(Hebrews 6:11-12)

Yours,

John Gillespie.

Notes:~

Love one another deeply, from the heart.
(1 Peter 1:22)

Let's Hear It For Climate Change!

Dear Church Family,

It is about time that I confess to you all a deep dark secret of mine. I am praying and hoping for Climate Change. I am expecting it. I am looking for things to heat up, and I am wanting to see some serious melting of ice. I want to see culture and commerce disrupted. I want to see levels rise. I want to see people having to make costly decisions because their world is changing. Climate Change sounds to me to be just the very thing that we need!

Of course, I am not speaking about the weather. I am speaking about seeing the spiritual temperature of the People of God raised. Whatever may be happening globally, I am concerned to see something happen spiritually that will transcend physical space and time. I am praying for a change in the *spiritual* climate first in Christ's Church, and then in the world around us.

I sometimes wonder if you would really want me as your pastor if you knew what I was praying for and looking for in regard to our lives together. If the Lord answers my prayer (and the prayers of many others) and we start seeing Spiritual Climate Change, then there is going to be some serious disruption around here. Let me try to get specific.

What is Spiritual Climate Change?

In brief, it is a new encounter with Jesus Christ. It happens when He, whose face is like the sun in its noonday strength, draws *near*. When a believer, or a company of believers, sees Jesus Christ in a new light, Climate Change is about to happen. The spiritual temperature is going to rise. Another name for what I am speaking about is *Revival*.

What will Spiritual Climate Change do?

Raise the spiritual temperature amongst the People of God. This means that we will no longer fit easily into a world that is happy with lukewarmness. People really don't mind if we are 'mildly religious'. But a heart that burns hot for Christ is another matter. Climate Change will cause us to love the Lord Jesus with a renewed fervency, and our raised temperature will inevitably radiate out in evangelism.

It will melt the ice in relationships among the People of God. When Christ draws near, believers grow in their love for each other. We see it in the Bible, but we shun it in experience. We are comfortable with relationships that are 'cool', but Christ wants us to 'love one another *deeply*, from the heart' (1 Peter 1:22). This is 'unBritish', but it is biblical... and it speaks to the frozen, lonely world of a new Kingdom fuelled by radical love-empowered relationships.

It will disrupt the culture and commerce among the People of God. Let's face it; we are too worldly. We often live in our little islands of comparative wealth and comfort and surround ourselves with our agendas just like the unbelieving world does. But Climate Change will change all of that. God's will can flood over us and drown our little worlds. Yes, we need to exist in and contribute to society; of course we do. But our sights should be higher than simply achieving personal peace and prosperity. God has more for us, but realising His dream will probably have to involve the washing away of our own.

Climate change will cause significant movement among the People of God. As the temperature rises, as the ice melts, and the level of God's love rises and drowns out our little worlds, we are going to become a People On The Move. Mission will be inevitable and unavoidable. Our minds and hearts will be set upon the Lord and His Kingdom *first*, and all else will take a back seat to what God's will is for us:

That we enjoy Him supremely and live for the spread of His fame in all the earth, for the joy of all peoples.

Will you pray for Climate Change? Do you see the urgent need for it? Are you longing to see Jesus Christ draw near to us? Are you seeking a warm... even a hot... heart of love for Him? Are you willing to have the ice melt between you and others? Are you ready for Him to disrupt *your* agenda and plans, flooding your life with *His*? Are you ready to migrate *out* with a heart for mission? These are the things that I am praying for, preaching for, longing for!

Let's join together in this.

Let's hunger together for Climate Change.

Yours,

John Gillespie.

Notes:~

For I am convinced that neither death nor life,
neither angels nor demons,
neither the present nor the future, nor any powers,
neither height nor depth,
nor anything else in all creation,
will be able to separate us from the love of God
that is in Christ Jesus our Lord.
(Romans 8:38-39)

Scale The Everest Heights!

Beloved in Christ,

Once again it is a joy to write to you and to encourage you in the Lord Jesus. It is my hope that we are growing in faith and confidence in Christ even in the midst of a culture that has seemingly lost its rudder.

Below is the famous passage that the apostle Paul penned for the saints in Rome. Those who first heard and read these words were living in a world on the brink of collapse. Rome was weary of its wealth and morally rotten to the core. Each successive Emperor grew more tyrannical. Christians were without question swimming against the tide of their times in their devotion to Christ and their refusal of the values of a godless society. I consider the passage below to be the 'Mount Everest' of the Bible, the very pinnacle of the Scriptures. Don't rush over it. Climb it slowly. Take time to view the world below from its lofty summit. It will do your soul immeasurable good.

Romans 8:38-39

And we know that in all things God works for the good of those who love Him, who have been called according to His purpose. For those God foreknew He also predestined to be conformed to the likeness of His Son, that He might be the firstborn among many brothers. And those He predestined, He also called; those He called, He also justified; those He justified, He also glorified.

What, then, shall we say in response to this? If God is for us, who can be against us? He who did not spare His own Son, but gave Him up for us all — how will He not also, along with Him, graciously give us all things? Who will bring any charge against those whom God has chosen? It is God who justifies. Who is he that condemns? Christ Jesus, who died — more than that, who was raised to life — is at the right hand of God and is also interceding for us. Who shall separate us from the love of Christ? Shall trouble or hardship or persecution or famine or nakedness or danger or sword? As it is written:

'For your sake we face death all day long; we are considered as sheep to be slaughtered.' No, in all these things we are more than conquerors through Him who loved us. For I am convinced that neither death nor life, neither angels nor demons, neither the present nor the future, nor any powers, neither height nor depth, nor anything else in all creation, will be able to separate us from the love of God that is in Christ Jesus our Lord.

Now, you simply cannot beat the truths offered in that passage! Look down upon life from such a vantage, and everything takes on a proper perspective. Here we see our salvation rooted in Eternity Past, and guaranteed into Eternity Future. Here we have a certainty that in the providence of an all-wise and all-good God *everything* is somehow being worked into His Eternal plan for our good and His glory. Here we find the astounding, joy-building, life-strengthening truth that *nothing* can separate the simple believer from Christ. Nothing... not a wicked Roman empire, not a disease, not a current financial meltdown... NOTHING.

Friends, if I did not believe in the power of Christ, and the surety of His Gospel, I would despair. I believe in a God who has sent His Son to die for us (the hard part) and will therefore not fail to keep us through all things until eternal life (the easy part).

So, having scaled the heights of Bible Truth, let's live in the valleys of this life with the confidence that only the Lord Jesus and His Gospel can give. Let's be sure that we are established in the Lord, not in stock-market, or our own health, or any other uncertainty.

This is the Life of Faith.

This is the Overcoming Life.

This is our Present Victory.

May the Lord Jesus Himself establish you as you put your confidence in Him alone.

Yours,

John Gillespie.

(Remember what *Mission* is? 'The purposeful taking of the Gospel across boundaries of unbelief.' Let's do it!)

Notes:~

Week 14

God is our refuge and our strength,
an ever-present help in trouble.
(Psalm 46:1)

Let's Get God's Perspective On Things

Dear Family in Christ,

[Written during a time of national economic crisis]

What a few weeks it has been! Everywhere we look we see things being shaken and the constant talk is of impending doom and gloom. If I did not know Jesus Christ, and if my joy was solely dependent upon the passing things of Earth, my happiness factor would be as up and down as the Stock Market. But it is not. I am upbeat because I believe in Jesus, and I have determined that *He* indeed is, and shall be, my treasure. I admit to you that I have to keep reminding myself of this, but by God's grace this I have determined to do.

Now, I believe that the Bible, being God's wholly sufficient Word, has something to say to us in virtually every instance of life. A key to spiritual stability and joy, regardless of circumstances, is found in developing the good habit of going to the Scriptures and asking the Lord; 'Lord, what do You have to say to me in the light of the particular situation I am being confronted with?' Without fail the Lord Jesus will speak to us in timeless truths through His Word.

So, here we find ourselves in a very real financial crisis. Do not underestimate the gravity of what we are going through. Our chickens are coming home to roost. Decades of living on the edge of, or beyond, our means has taken its toll on the very soundness of our financial institutions. We have wanted to 'have it all' and 'right now'. What our grandparents only dreamed of, we have demanded. What were once considered luxuries are now necessities; a car (or two), buying a house, wall-to-wall carpet, a holiday every year... What our parents worked their entire lives to acquire, we now expect from the start. None of us really knows how deep the crisis will take us. Perhaps the government 'bail outs' and 'prop ups' will close the wounds and stem the flow, but perhaps not. *Scary times...!*

As Christians, we are called to seek the Lord's counsel in all of this. We are to go to Him in His Word, get His perspective on things and respond accordingly. There are countless Scriptural passages that apply to our current situation, some of them comforting, some of them devastating in their indictment of our idolatry. I feel it right to offer a passage of comfort to us all, one which is designed to lift our sights above the turmoil and give us strength. Let's let Psalm 46 speak to us right now:

God is our refuge and our strength,
an ever-present help in trouble.
Therefore we will not fear, though the earth give way
and the mountains fall into the heart of the sea,

though its waters roar and foam
and the mountains quake with their surging.
Selah

There is a river whose streams make glad the city of God,
the holy place where the Most High dwells.

God is within her, she will not fall;
God will help her at break of day.

Nations are in uproar, kingdoms fall;
He lifts his voice, the earth melts.

The LORD Almighty is with us;
the God of Jacob is our fortress.
Selah

Come and see the works of the LORD,
the desolations He has brought on the earth.
He makes wars cease to the ends of the earth;
He breaks the bow and shatters the spear,
He burns the shields with fire.

'Be still, and know that I am God;
I will be exalted among the nations,
I will be exalted in the earth.'

The LORD Almighty is with us;
the God of Jacob is our fortress.
Selah

Just notice with me the strengthening truths of this great Psalm. It begins with an affirmation that *God* is our source of peace and security *in the midst of calamity*, and goes on to assert His absolute sovereignty over the affairs of men and nations. The Psalm uses poetry to paint a picture of the complete collapse of one's world: mountains quaking and surging; the seas foaming; the very earth giving way beneath us! Pretty bad! But just behold the contrast:

> There is a river whose streams make glad the city of God,
> the holy place where the Most High dwells.

> God is within her, she will not fall;
> God will help her at break of day.

Far above the surging waves and quaking mountains is a peaceful river and a glad city. *God* is enthroned there... this city rests secure, above the calamity below. *Believers are citizens of this city!* The Psalm presents God as sovereign over storming nations and bids believers to:

> 'Be still, and know that I am God;
> I will be exalted among the nations,
> I will be exalted in the earth.'

Now, believing friends, it is our *duty* to place our joys in that Heavenly City. We are *called* to be people of faith even in times of fear. It is not an option... this is our faith! Troubled times are an opportunity for believers in Jesus to live and act as people with Hope. We have an answer for a world in crisis.

Let's be in the holy habit of strengthening ourselves in the Lord. Let's not allow ourselves to wallow in fear and faithlessness. Let's be those who get God's perspective on things and who live as citizens of a secure, Heavenly City. I have no inside knowledge on what will happen to our economy; what may happen in our environment; what might take place between warring nations. But I know that Jesus Christ is my Lord and Saviour, the God of History, the Sovereign One. In Him we rest secure.

> The LORD Almighty is with us;
> the God of Jacob is our fortress.

Yours,

John Gillespie.

Notes:~

Week 15

Blessed are those whose strength is in You...
(Psalm 84:5)

Let's Not Fit In!

Beloved in Christ,

[Written during a time of national economic crisis]

Peter addressed the Christians of his day as 'strangers in the world' (1 Peter 1:1). Because we believe that the Word of God is timeless, such a title must be appropriate for us today as well. But, let's be honest with one another... it sounds more like another 'religion' than what we are involved in today... perhaps from another planet or time dimension.

Strangers?

Elsewhere we are referred to as 'pilgrims'. To modern ears this sounds perhaps even more bizarre than strangers. It conjures up images of weird people in long black frocks with dour faces and with hats on. The last thing most of us want to be are 'strangers in the world', or out-of-place 'pilgrims'. Likewise, a 'pilgrim' is someone on a journey of faith. Neither strangers nor pilgrims feel at home where they are. Both are looking elsewhere for their rest, joy and fullness.

We want to have it all, right now. We've been trained to be this way. We consider such to be our birthright. For many of us Jesus Christ is just a means to an end... a way to get what we want out of life. That is one reason why the present economic trouble is so distressing to some of us. It may infringe upon our happiness here below (I realise too that there are deeper, and better, reasons to be concerned about the current economic crisis). But let's just let these two descriptions of what in fact we *are* as Christians press their full weight upon us.

Pilgrims.

Strangers.

These words are meant to describe us. They are vivid with meaning. They are liberating and exciting. They speak of a people on the move; a people with vision and hope. These words

52

are meant to put the world into perspective and help us to understand our proper place in it. I want us to try for just a moment to remove from these words negative images of long-faced, nearly miserable folk trudging along a dusty path. To help us gain insight into just what it means for us to be 'strangers' and 'pilgrims' on earth I want to call on some help from the Psalmist.

'Blessed are those whose strength is in You,
who have set their hearts on pilgrimage.
As they pass through the Valley of Baca,
They make it a place of springs...
They go on from strength to strength,
till each appears before God in Zion.'

The 'Valley of Baca' means the 'Valley of Weeping'. It is representative of this sad world. Just look at what those 'strangers' on 'pilgrimage' do as they travel through this valley... Having their hearts set upon appearing before God, and gaining their strength from the Lord, and not from this arid world, they actually transform the desert valley into a 'place of springs'. There is undoubtedly a joy in these sojourners. This is not a morbid procession, but a joyous throng. Their hearts are set upon the Lord; their strength is from Him, and they are world changers. They are joy-spreaders.

Notice also that these sojourners are being transformed even as they are travelling. 'They go on from strength to strength...' The world, of which we are called to be 'strangers', produces exactly the opposite effect upon those who find themselves 'at home' in it. It wearies its citizens. It wears out those who settle in it. In contrast this pilgrim procession is gaining power with every step.

I want to be a part of this company! Without a doubt, 'strangers' and 'pilgrims' may have to pay a high price for not fitting into this weary, wayward world. But the price is worth it. This heaven-bound company are both changing their world and being changed along the way.

Are you 'at home' in this world as it is? Are you a settler or a sojourner? Are you looking for your dreams to be fulfilled in this Valley of Weeping? I want to invite you to become a pilgrim. I want to call you to become a stranger in this world. Join with me... and millions of others, who have set their hearts on another country... a heavenly one. Watch... *and see* what a difference you will make and what a difference will be made in you.

Let's not fit in!

Yours,

John Gillespie.

Notes:~

Progress and joy in the faith.
(Philippians 1:25)

Faith's Fitness Centre

Dear Grace Family,

Have you ever considered the fact that faith is like a muscle that must be exercised if it is to grow? Faith's focus is Jesus Christ, and Jesus Christ alone, and while I would rather have a weak and feeble faith in Christ than faith (be it ever so strong) in anything else... nevertheless, there is value in a strong and mature faith in Jesus Christ. Faith can grow or shrink, depending upon our exercise of it.

The Apostle Paul wrote to the Corinthian Christians:
'Our hope is that... your faith continues to grow...'
(2 Corinthians 10:15)

He wrote to the Philippians:

'Progress and joy in the faith.' (Philippians 1:25)

Paul was thankful to God for the saints in Thessalonica because:

'[their] faith [was] growing more and more.'
(2 Thessalonians 1:3)

I could marshal many more Scriptures to establish my case for faith growing and developing, but I think that the above proves the fact.

Now, if faith is meant to grow and develop, if indeed it is likened to a muscle that strengthens with use or weakens without, then clearly we should take time regularly to put our faith in Christ through its paces in order to develop it. One's ability to trust, increasingly, Christ for *all things* should be developing as surely as our physical fitness (assuming we apply ourselves to getting fit). But here we find a problem. In the same way that many of us do not keep our bodies fit, many of us simply do not exercise our faith. Okay, we 'officially' trust in Christ as Saviour. But then we stop there! We often shun challenges that require active faith in Christ to surmount, and in so doing we remain weaklings, spiritually unfit.

But perhaps you are asking: 'What difference does it make? As long as I get to Heaven, what difference does it make if I remain a spiritual baby now?' I bet your wife or husband could give you a few good answers to that question, but we will let the Bible provide three clear, quick answers. Each answer will relate to the three Scriptures I gave you above:

1. As (*only* as) our faith in Christ *grows*, the work of the Gospel expands to regions beyond us. Boundaries of unbelief are crossed as we mature:

'Our hope is that as your faith continues to grow... we can preach the Gospel *in regions beyond you*.' (2 Corinthians 10:15,16)

2. Our present *joy* is directly linked to our progress in faith. If we remain joyless and downcast, it is a sure sign of the unfitness of our faith:

'...I will continue with all of you for your progress and *joy* in the faith. (Philippians 1:25)

3. Our love for one another is index linked to the development of our faith in Christ. A loveless Church is a faithless Church. A loving Church is a Church where the saints are being active in their faith:

'...because your faith is growing more and more and the love you have for one another is increasing.' (2 Thessalonians 1:3)

So we see here that the development of our faith is no small matter. Mission, joy and love are directly linked to it. As faith grows, or shrinks, so do these.

Therefore, allow me to put you on a treadmill for just a moment in order to test the fitness of your faith. I want you to ask yourself just four questions, and I want you to answer them frankly and honestly.

1. When was the last time I dared to ask God for the impossible in prayer (the healing of an illness; the overthrow of an oppressive regime etc)?

2. Am I believing God for real present holiness, a change of my character into Christ-likeness, or am I just giving up and expecting those around me to continue putting up with my selfishness?

3. Am I 'seeking first the Kingdom of God' with my time, finances, hopes and dreams, trusting that God *really will* meet all of my needs as I seek to have my treasure in Christ?

4. Am I still trusting for the salvation of lost loved ones, praying earnestly for them, asking God for courage to speak up about Christ when the opportunity arises, standing upon the promises in God's Word for their salvation, or have I in reality given up?

Enough! I could suggest plenty more questions, but some of you are looking pretty out of breath already.

Is it time to get back into Faith's Fitness Centre?

Brothers and Sisters, let's be a *believing people*. Let's not read about movements, let's *be a movement*. Begin small if you have to, but work up, until you (we) are trusting Christ for *every detail of life... and even for our generation*. Let's get back to being praying people... who bring *everything* to Christ and *look to Him* for blessing, provision, miracle.

I leave you to catch your breath with a faith-filled quote from one of my heroes, William Carey:

'Attempt great things for God...

Expect great things FROM God'

Yours,

John Gillespie.

Notes:~

Week 17

*Do not conform any longer to the pattern of this world,
but be transformed by the renewing of your mind.
(Romans 12:2)*

A Formula That Works

Dear Friends,

One of the most frequently asked questions that I receive in my Pastor's study is: 'How can I discover God's will for my life?'

This simple but vexing question is of profound importance for all followers of Jesus Christ, not only for those in their teens and early twenties, but for all disciples at every stage of life.

Now, I don't want to underestimate the gravity of the question, nor to over-simplify the way toward a sure answer, but I really do believe that there is a 'formula' for discovering the will of God in our lives that is all but failure-proof. I am going to give you the formula, then show you the Scripture from which it is derived, and then *encourage you to apply it in your life.*

Here is the 'formula':

Worship — Worldliness + God's Word = Discovery of God's Will

Here's the Scripture:

Therefore, I urge you brothers, in view of God's mercy to offer your bodies as living sacrifices, holy and pleasing to God — this is your spiritual service of worship. Do not conform any longer to the pattern of this world, but be transformed by the renewing of your mind. Then you will be able to test and approve what God's will is — His good, pleasing and perfect will.
(Romans 12: 1-2)

Now, if you take a careful look at the passage above, you will see the 'equation' or 'formula' very clearly in it. Go ahead and take some time right now to hunt for it...

...Do you see it?

...It really is very clear, and makes great sense.

Just in case you haven't found it, let me help you.

In the passage, written by the Apostle Paul to the Christians in Rome, Paul is urging the Roman Christians to respond to the wonders of the Gospel:

Therefore, in view of God's mercy...

1. Offer your bodies as living sacrifices to God - this is your spiritual act of worship.

Here is the first part of the equation: *Worship; the offering of our living selves to God, not holding anything back, not striking any bargains, but placing ourselves and our lives every day on the altar of worship as a lifestyle.* So we have:

Worship

2. Do not conform any longer to the pattern of this world.

Here is the next part of the formula. *Refuse to be shaped by the values of the world around you. Literally 'do not let the world squeeze you into its mould'. Say 'no' to the self-centred, me-first values of a fallen society.* Now we have:

Worship — Worldliness

Now we add: *But be transformed by the renewing of your mind. Allow God's Word to have its way in reshaping you from the core out. Get your mind thinking the way God thinks by getting His Word into you.* So now we have:

Worship — Worldliness + God's Word

Then we will be: *Able to discover God's will. His wonderful (good), satisfying (pleasing) and fulfilling (perfect) will.* See it?

Worship — Worldliness + God's Word = Discovery of God's Will

Now, each part of the equation is of vital importance! You cannot change the formula. For instance, if you want to discover God's will (wanting the joy and fulfilment that comes from being where God wants you to be), but refuse to 'present your body as a living sacrifice' (Worship), insisting on living for yourself instead of Christ, the formula falls apart. If you want to be in the centre of God's will, but also insist on holding to your worldly values of 'me first' (Worldliness), the equation simply won't add up.

So! There you have it. A straightforward answer to an age-old question... clear as it can be and right in the Bible. God has a will for each of our lives, a purpose that fits us, a reason to live that fulfils us and gives Him glory. Plug your life into the equation, and... dare I say... I *guarantee* that you will discover your very purpose for living in this year, next year... and beyond. There is no other reasonable response for the Jesus Christ for a believer.

Oh, by the way, it works for families and churches too! Let's do it together!

Yours,

John Gillespie.

Notes:~

And we who with unveiled faces all contemplate the Lord's glory...
(2 Corinthians 3:18)

No 'Click... Whoosh...' With God

Dear Brothers and Sisters,

Let me tell you a story.

I began my life as a pastor in the very rural stretches of Arkansas, in the Deep South of the USA... swamps, mosquitoes, snakes, coyotes and country people, some of whom had cleared their own land with their own hands. Folks lived in homes they had built from timber they had felled and sawn themselves. I could tell you tales of fried chicken, raccoon hunting, and old time 'revival meetings' for hours.

But the story (fable) is told of one old-time family... Pa, Ma, and 'Junior' (thirty-five years old, and still living at home on the farm), and their once-in-a-life-time excursion into the 'big city' (Little Rock)...

Imagine with me this old-time country family squeezing into the front seat of their old pick-up truck, driving down the old farm lane, onto the gravel road (Pa always preferred gravel to pavements), excitedly, nervously on their way to the city. Pa and Ma, now well on in years, had never made such a trip, and figured it was time to give Junior a taste of the big-wide world.

Before long they turned onto the paved road and then finally onto Highway 40 towards Little Rock (Junior had never been as far as Highway 40 before). With each passing mile the family's eyes grew wider and wider as the city grew closer and closer. Imagine their wonder as they entered the city! At every turn were sights and sounds and smells never seen and experienced before!

Planning on an overnight stay, they had it in mind to check into a hotel (Pa had stayed in the Sunset Inn in Hope once, but never in a 'city' hotel). Turning their old pick-up into the drive of the Hilton, their breath nearly left them as they took in the grandeur of the place...

They parked the truck in front of the entryway...

Pa said: 'Ma, you wait here in the truck while Junior and I go inside and fetch us a room.'

Ma waited as the men walked through the revolving doors (a totally new experience for both of them). Once inside Pa and Junior took a few minutes simply to stare and try to take it all in. On their left, they heard a strange noise...

Click... Whoosh... Click... Whoosh...

Turning to see, they beheld the strangest sight their country eyes had ever seen. Here were two shiny metal doors. Someone would come up beside them, press a lighted button, wait a moment, and... Click... Whoosh... the shiny metal doors would open... into a little room they would step, then... Click... Whoosh, the shiny doors would close. Then... Click... Whoosh, the shiny doors would open and out of the little room would step what looked like totally different people!

As Pa and Junior watched in wonder and bewilderment, up to the shiny metal doors came an old woman, about Ma's age. She pressed the lighted button and waited a minute.

Click... Whoosh... opened the doors and into the little room she stepped. Click... Whoosh... the doors to the little room closed. Pa watched. Junior held his breath. Sure enough, a minute later... Click... Whoosh.... to Pa's amazement out stepped a beautiful 25-year-old blonde lady!

'Quick!' said Pa, elbowing Junior. 'Go get Ma!'

Wouldn't it be wonderful if our transformation was that simple! It isn't, but the transformation that Christ offers is not that shallow either. His goal is not just to change us on the surface, but down to the core. His work is from the inside out:

Our Character...
Our Motivation...
Our Values...
Our Purpose for living...

In an age where image is valued above substance and cosmetics are deemed more important than character, what Jesus Christ has to offer may well be disregarded by many who want change at a 'Click... Whoosh...' level. Christ wants to make us holy. He aims to fashion our hearts to be like His. This may, indeed will, involve...

            Painful times...
               Trials...
                    Patient endurance...
                  Decades...

But the work He does will be lasting, valuable, deep, world-impacting, eternity-enriching.

Brothers and Sisters, let's invite Him to do a deeper work in us. Let's open up ourselves to the Lord Jesus and let Him demolish and remake us into conformity with Himself. I leave you with a glorious Scripture to meditate on:

And we who with unveiled faces all contemplate the Lord's glory are being...transformed into His likeness with ever-increasing glory, which comes from the Lord, who is the Spirit.
(2 Corinthians 3:18)

Blessings,

John Gillespie.

Notes:~

Let no debt remain outstanding, except the continuing debt to love one another,
for he who loves his fellow man has fulfilled the law.
(Romans 13:8)

The Debt We Can Never Pay Off

Dear Church,

Take just a minute and chew on the Scripture text at the top of this page. It is no news to you for me to tell you that we are hearing a lot these days about debt, and most of what we hear is pretty disheartening. We are hearing every day about bad debts, the debt crisis, debt consolidation, etc. etc. etc. People are putting themselves in impossible situations because they want to 'have it all'... now.

But I want us to focus on the form of debt described in the passage from Romans above. Notice that the Bible here clearly states that as Christians we are to faithfully pay off all earthly, financial debts: 'Let no debt remain outstanding...' But then notice that there is another form of debt, not financial, to which every Christian has an obligation:
> '...the continuing debt to love one another...'

I just want to highlight three things about this form of debt:

1. It is a *reasonable* obligation, for we are empowered by Jesus Christ to fulfil it. We do not seek to love one another in our own strength, through our own meagre resources, which would quickly be depleted. When we try to love in our own power, we run the risk of bankruptcy.

2. It is an *ongoing* obligation, for it is a continuing debt. With this world's debts you can pay them off, or default on them, or declare bankruptcy, but with the debt to love each other we discover an ongoing debt which we can never pay off. We can never get to the place where we say, 'I have loved you enough... I can stop now. Your turn...'

3. It is an *universal* obligation, for we are to love one another. Some are easier to love than others, but 'one another' sets no boundaries to our debt of love. 'One another' implies those we enjoy loving, and those who give us nothing in return. This requires an endless 'bank' from which we can draw, and that bank is Jesus Himself and His boundless store of grace.

Well, regardless of what the economy does, regardless of your personal financial blessings or woes, we are all in debt to one another, to love one another with the love of Jesus Christ. Let's seek grace (*boundless* grace!) to fulfil the 'unfulfillable'... our debt of love to those around us. Begin with your nearest neighbours... your spouse, and family, then move out to your church and community. In so doing we will be a greater witness to the world than ever we could imagine.

Jesus said: 'By this shall all men know that you are My disciples: if you have love one for another.'

Grace and peace to you in all abundance through our Lord and Saviour Jesus Christ.

Yours,

John Gillespie.

Notes:~

*Go home to your family and tell them how much the Lord
has done for you, and how He has had mercy on you.
(Mark 5:19)*

The Toughest Assignment

Dear Church Family,

The words above were spoken by the Lord Jesus to a man from
whom He had just delivered a whole host of demons. You can read
about the entire event in Mark, chapter five.

Having just been set free from forces that had controlled his life,
perhaps for all of his life, he understandably wanted to follow
Jesus from henceforth wherever Jesus went. But Jesus would not
let him. Instead, He told him to do something that is arguably the
toughest assignment in the Christian life: to 'go home to your
family and tell them how much the Lord has done for you, and how
He has had mercy on you.'

I think we will all admit that our families are perhaps the toughest
mission fields of all. They know all about us! They have seen us at
our worst. What a task Jesus assigns this newly converted, freshly
delivered man! Could he not go to Bible School first with Jesus and
the disciples and then, a few years down the road, perhaps after
founding some great ministry (i.e. 'Demoniacs Anonymous'),
achieving some fame, proving himself, go and give the Gospel in
power to Mum and Dad?

No, Jesus sent him straight away, with nothing but the power of his
testimony of God's grace in his life. Notice what Jesus did not tell
him to say or do:

Go home and...
Impress them with how much Bible knowledge you now have...
Amaze them with your new found super-spirituality...
Tell them they are all going to hell if they do not become
like you...
Promise them that you'll never mess up again...

No, the assignment was simple and fool-proof:

Go home and tell...
What the Lord has done for you...
How He has had mercy on you...

In other words... give them your testimony, but make it a Christ-centred testimony. Tell of God's goodness to your needy soul. Speak of God's grace to a ruined man. There is perhaps little so powerful as a testimony of God's grace. It can even work on family members!

I am sometimes concerned that when we have new encounters with the Lord, perhaps at a conference, or some such event, we develop a sense of spiritual superiority. The last thing we have in mind is our family, or perhaps our Church family. We want to leave such stragglers behind and move on in a new circle of spiritual experience. But the Lord Jesus may not want us to do that! He may say to us just what He said to the delivered man!

'Go home' (back to your kindred, or back to your local church).
'Bless others by telling of My goodness to you.'
'Speak not of their inadequacy, but of My mercy.'
'See what I can do through you in the toughest mission field of all... your own back yard!'

What was the result of this man's return to his home town?

'The man began to tell how much Jesus had done for him...
And all the people were amazed.'

Let's live for the fame of Christ, even with our families, church families and friends.

Blessings in Jesus,

John Gillespie.

Notes:~

Jesus said, 'I am...the Truth...'
(John 14:6)

The Absolute Truth That We Need

Dear Church Family,

In a small factory town in Bavaria there once lived a clockmaker. In his shop's front window, facing the town's Fore street, stood the grandfather clock that he had made years before when apprenticing for his trade.

Every day workmen bustled past his shop on their way to and from work in the factory. Over time, the watchmaker began to notice that each and every morning a particular man, better dressed than those rushing to work alongside him, would stop and set his pocket watch to the time on the old grandfather's clock in the window. Days and weeks went by and the months turned into years. Every day the well-dressed man stopped to go through his time-keeping routine.

Finally the old watchmaker ventured outside to enquire of the man, 'Say there! Every day I see you stopping by my shop to set your pocket watch by my clock in the window. Why? What's your purpose in needing to be so exact?'

'Well,' said the well-dressed man, 'You see, I am the manager at the factory, and among other things, it is my job to blow the whistle every day at precisely 5pm to signal an end to the work day. The whole town relies on that whistle being accurate. This old pocket watch of mine never has kept good time... and I rely on your fine clock to give me the correct time. Thanks to your clock I can blow the all-important whistle on time!'

'Oh dear,' said the red-faced old clockmaker, 'we have a problem! You see, that old grandfather clock you rely on never has kept good time either. Every day I set its time by your factory whistle!'

The little story above illustrates very well the results of living without an absolute from which to measure all other areas of life. We can't live without standards, and we cannot have standards without a Standard from which to judge and weigh all else. PROBLEM: We live in an age which eschews any notion of absolute truth from which we can judge right and wrong and to which we can appeal. The last verse of the ancient book of Judges pretty well sums up our age:

> 'In those days there was no king in the land...
> everyone did as he saw fit in his own eyes.'
> (Judges 21:25)

In ancient Israel Relativism ruled and chaos flourished! So it seems to be in our day. When there is no 'king'; that is, no agreed standard of judgement, everyone is left to be their own little king; that is, to determine truth as it suits them, to formulate standards that fit their own desires.

But the very freedoms we so cherish are built upon an agreed understanding that there is a higher law, above us, outside of us, whose origin is in the character of God Himself, from which we derive our values and make our choices, and to which we are all accountable.

The freedom to live free from tyranny, to govern oneself, is entirely dependent upon a common conviction that there is Absolute Truth that ultimately sits in judgement above us all. But if the clockmaker's clock keeps time badly, then all the pocket watches in town are set to the wrong time! Anarchy rules where Truth doesn't!

Over the past generation, we have watched our lawmakers steadily overthrow laws that were founded upon the common belief that there was a God from whom all true Law comes. We have allowed our schools and universities to teach our young minds that 'there is no such a thing as absolute truth' (that popular claim contradicts itself... can you see how?). We ourselves have often marginalised God and His Truth, in favour of our own self interests. The Church has often been no more faithful in keeping a plumb-line for Truth in society than was that old clockmaker's clock faithful in setting a reliable time for the town to run by.

Beloved, if our society is to survive, then the Church (that's you and me!) needs to believe and declare to our 'kingless' generation that there is a King; there is Truth (with a capital 'T'); there is a God who speaks, and feels, and hears, and sees, and saves, and judges. This is our calling and our charge. We need to live under the Lordship of Christ ourselves, and then call our generation to live under His Lordship with us. The only other option will be the destruction of society as we know it, and the loss of our very freedom, so rare and once cherished.

Pray and ask The Lord to give you fresh courage to live under the wonderful Lordship of Jesus Christ, that together we might make choices and cherish values which reflect His Truth. Flee moral compromise, and avoid the temptation to 'fit in' to a world which refuses to acknowledge that there is a God of Truth who governs all things. Ask God for a new courage to witness to a rudderless world.

There is no other hope for our world than the Truth that is in Jesus Christ.

Grace and Peace,

John Gillespie.

Notes:~

God promises to meet all our needs...
(Philippians 4:19)

God's Guarantees

Dear Family,

I feel a need to bring a little clarification to something that I emphasised from the pulpit last Sunday morning. [For the readers of this book, I have been preaching through the book of Revelation.]

You may recall that I said that the only thing that I can guarantee you as your pastor is deliverance from the wrath of God through the power of the shed blood of Christ. I cannot guarantee you health, financial advancement, temporal success, etc.

Now, for the most part, I really do stand by that statement. Overall, I think it is true. I think its truth is found everywhere in the Scriptures. Believers, who have been truly delivered from the righteous wrath of God through the blood of His Son, do not always fare well here on Earth. There is not only *not* a guarantee that they will always fare well, there are actually many promises that suffering and hardship await true believers this side of Heaven. God is not a salesman who only tells us what we want to hear. He tells us the truth even down to the 'fine print', and the Bible makes the reality of persecution and trials for God's children abundantly plain. I could provide many scriptures to prove my point, but I think you already agree with me, and some of those scriptures are probably already coming to your minds.

But, there are some other wonderful things that God guarantees to us, and we should not fail to be mindful of such things.

He promises His presence with us always:
'Never will I leave you;
never will I forsake you.' So we say with confidence,
'The Lord is my helper; I will not be afraid.
What can man do to me?' (Hebrews 13:5-6)

He promises sufficient grace for all circumstances:
'My grace is sufficient for you, for My power
is made perfect in weakness.'
(2 Corinthians 12:9)

He promises to change us and to not give up the project until we are holy:
[H]e who began a good work in you will carry it on to completion until the day of Christ Jesus. (Philippians 1:6)

And you may bring to mind other guarantees in which believers can and should rejoice. But we should bear in mind that all these other guarantees are in place because we have been delivered from God's wrath, saved and sealed, by the blood of Christ. That is the wellspring from which all other blessings flow. Hence, Paul says: He who did not spare His own Son, but gave Him up for us all — how will He not also, along with Him, graciously give us all things? (Romans 8:33)

But, furthermore, there are many, many blessings in this Christian life which, while not being 'guaranteed' in the same sense of our salvation through Christ (that is, absolutely, sure, by virtue of the blood of Christ, and received without question by a simple act of faith), are nevertheless there for us in Christ to believe in, and fight in faith for. We will impoverish ourselves if we fail to see the many precious promises that God has for us as His children. For example:

God promises to meet all our needs:
And my God will meet all your needs according
to His glorious riches in Christ Jesus. (Philippians 4:19)

God invites us to pray in faith for impossible situations and believe for great results:
Now to Him who is able to do immeasurably more than all we ask or imagine, according to His power that is at work within us...
(Ephesians 3:20)

God wills for us to pray in faith for the sick and ask in faith for their healing:#
Is any one of you sick? He should call the elders of
the church to pray over him and
anoint him with oil in the name of the Lord.
And the prayer offered in faith will make
the sick person well; the Lord will raise him up.
If he has sinned, he will be forgiven. (James 5:14,15)

God offers us joy and abundance in life through Jesus Christ: 'I
have come that they might have life, and have it to the full.'
(John 10:10)

And, again, there are many other very precious promises in the Word of God for us to rejoice in, receive, and act upon. Yes, some 'health and wealth' teachers have abused such promises in order to feed their (and our) greed and lust, but that does not mean that we should not benefit from the abundance offered us in God's Word as His children.

As we live under the Great Guarantee of deliverance from wrath through the Blood of Jesus Christ, please let's be encouraged to 'press in' with the very many and precious promises of God for His Church. How tragic if we live like paupers when God wills us to live as sons of the King! May the Lord lead us to new frontiers of faith where we are trusting Him in new ways, and in new areas.

With eyes fixed confidently on Eternity, let's live boldly by faith during our brief sojourn here in Time.

Yours, for Christ's Glory,

John Gillespie.

I know that praying for the sick is challenging to faith, and often raises many questions regarding God's sovereignty, but I am happily committed to this ministry because 1: God encourages it and 2: God never fails to bring blessing to the saints and glory to Himself even if He deems it right to heal through death or give grace for prolonged suffering. Such an attitude toward God's sovereignty does not reflect a 'cop out' by those who hold it, but a deep confidence (faith) in the character of God.

Notes:~

*Praise be to the God and Father of our Lord Jesus Christ,
the Father of compassion and the God of all comfort,
who comforts us in all our troubles, so that we can comfort
those in any trouble with the comfort we ourselves have received
from God. For just as the sufferings of Christ flow over into our
lives, so also through Christ our comfort overflows.*
(2 Corinthians 1:3-5)

Don't Waste Your Trials!

Dear Brothers and Sisters,

I want to encourage us today with a powerful truth from the Word of
God. It is a truth that has the power to transform situations where
pain and suffering seem to be overwhelming.

The Scripture passage above gives a value to suffering that
transforms it from a lonely, forsaken road of anguish to a meaningful
avenue of ministry. The passage tells us that suffering and pain
('troubles') actually have a redeeming quality to them that delivers
the sufferer from the double tragedy of suffering with futility to the
redemptive tragedy of suffering with purpose.

Explore the passage with me, and I am sure that you will see this
glorious truth as I and countless other followers of Jesus have.
Notice first of all that the Apostle Paul adopts an attitude of praise
to God, the 'Father of Compassion, and the God of all comfort', not
because God has prevented suffering from coming his way, but
because He has 'comforted [him] in all [his] troubles'. The ancient
Apostle does not have a rose-coloured view of life. He is realistic.
Life can be tough, but God, our compassionate Father, comforts His
children in the midst of the suffering.

But the sentence then delivers to us the truth that can be
revolutionary for the one caught in the current of a troublesome
time:

'...[God] comforts us in all our troubles so that we can comfort
those in any trouble with the comfort we ourselves have received
from God.'

Here then is the redemptive power of suffering that delivers the
sufferer from suffering with futility. Our sufferings, when combined
with the comforts which we have received from the 'God of all

74

comfort'... (get this)... enable us to become agents of comfort to those around us who are caught in the currents of their own sufferings.

This transforming truth gives us a clue as to why the Lord Jesus allows His own very dear children to pass through various, sometimes painful, and often prolonged, trials. Such experiences open up avenues of ministry that would otherwise be closed. If Christians walked only flower-strewn pathways of ease, the suffering world around them would be road-blocked to them. It is precisely because a believer has walked some sorrowful path, and discovered grace there in some new way, that he can relate to and minister to a fallen world around him. Understanding this delivers the suffering saint from the further pain of seeing their trials as futile. Trials in the life of a sanctified servant can be redeemed to become openings for ministry.

A message that cascades from this truth comes in the form of a warning: Christian! Don't waste trials! Allow them to drive you nearer and nearer to your Lord Jesus. Allow them to uproot you from the world and to re-plant you deep in the God of all comfort. A believer wastes his trials when he kicks against God while under them. They fail to do their good work in the saint's life if he complains against God rather than submitting to the Master's hand. Submit to the Lord in them.

Pray and ask Him to make you a greater blessing to a hurting world because these trials have come upon you.

Believer, for all the joys of this life, for all of the sunny days given to us to enjoy, we are not offered a life totally free from the tribulations common to our fallen race. God has designed it this way so that we can reach into the suffering world around us with the comfort we have received. We could multiply stories of God's grace spreading to a hurting world through the comforting ministries of suffering saints. Praise God for His amazing work in and through our lives!

Grace and Peace to all who love the Lord Jesus,

John Gillespie.

Notes:~

Week 24

A light unto my path.
(Psalm 119:105)

An Inexhaustible Mine Of Treasure

Dear Brothers and Sisters in Christ,

I value and cherish the Bible as God's Word almost above anything else on earth. I would choose a Bible over any earthly possession. I want to tell you why.

God speaks to me through His perfect Word. I really believe that. In a world of 1,000 voices all calling for and demanding my attention, I believe that the God of Eternity addresses me personally, and the Church collectively, through the Book of books, the Bible. When I take time to open God's Book, and when I humbly ask the Holy Spirit to shine upon the sacred page, God speaks to me through the written word as surely as if He were sitting next to me. He shows me Jesus Christ in His Word. He feeds my soul through His Word. He chastens, comforts, and guides me though His Word. Indeed, I understand the sentiments of the Psalmist who, when speaking of God's written Word, said:

Thy word is a lamp unto my feet, and a light unto my path.
(Psalm 119:105)
and
The entrance of thy words gives light; it gives understanding unto the simple. (Psalm 119:130)

The Bible is for me, a sure Word, and an inexhaustible mine of treasure that ministers Jesus Christ to my mind and soul day in and day out, year in and year out. Now, I know that the Bible has taken its knocks through the centuries, but it simply does not stay on the canvas. It keeps getting on its feet again, and is never down and out for the count. One of the great (but not good) Emperors of Rome (I think it was Julian) said 'destroy those Christians... and their book!' He was not able to do either, nor has anyone else since, nor will anyone hence.

One of the great challenges to the Bible today, however, is coming from right within the camp. It is not the Roman Emperor, or some boasting atheist who is launching the greatest and most dangerous attack on the Word of God. I fear that the greatest and most dangerous attack may well be arising from those who, one would

76

believe, would be the most passionate about the Word of God. The attack is most sinister in its subtlety. Perhaps there is nothing so threatening to the life of the Word of God in the midst of the People of God as the growing neglect of the Bible among those who claim to be believing followers of Jesus Christ... US.

Now, here is a truly strange situation: A people who claim to be hungry for the Lord (or so we say in our songs), and who long for intimacy with Jesus Christ (or so we say in our prayers), who want guidance in life so as to do the will of God (or so we say to one another), but who can and often do go days or more at a time with our Bibles closed and collecting dust in some forgotten corner of our lives and homes... and then, just to add a bit more irony, some of us will long for some 'word from the Lord' from another source.

Let me finish the warning, and then get back to encouraging. To expect God to speak to us while we neglect His Word is pure presumption. To expect genuine intimacy with the Christ of Time and Eternity (and not some invented idol of our own fanciful imaginations) while our Bibles sit closed under a stack of magazines, is wishing for the impossible. Christians who marginalise the Bible in their daily lives do more to endanger their species than the tyrants of Rome and their successors could ever do.

When we claim to be Bible Believers but live to a large degree in daily neglect of God's precious Word, we do more to marginalise God's Truth in society than Richard Dawkins and his merry band of atheists ever will. We need to cherish God's Word if we expect to survive. We need to cherish God's Word if we expect God's Word to have influence in the society around us.

And His Word is worth cherishing!

Countless millions of simple believers, over twenty centuries and in every corner of the world, can testify to the sufficiency of the Bible to bring them into a rich, growing, life-transforming relationship with the Living God.

Pray and ask God to give you a new hunger for the Bible.
Stretch yourself and start memorising Scriptures.
Seek to be diligent in a daily quiet time with the Lord.
Read the Bible to your family.
Ask God to show you Jesus Christ in the Scriptures.
Rediscover what GOD can do in your life through His wonderful Word.

One last thing: I and my colleagues are committed to being Bible men. We have no other calling than to minister Jesus Christ to you from the pages of the Scriptures... PLEASE PRAY FOR US AS WE SEEK TO BE FAITHFUL SERVANTS OF GOD'S WORD.

Yours,

John Gillespie.

Notes:~

*The man who formerly persecuted us is now preaching
the faith he once tried to destroy.
(Galatians 1:23)*

Don't Give Up!

Dear Family,

My wife Tessa and I are reading Jonathan Aitken's biography of John Newton together. We are being much encouraged by the amazing story of the man who wrote, among other hymns, 'Amazing Grace'. What is most amazing to us is the tracking of the work of God's Grace over the course of Newton's life... from slave trader to saint. This guy was bad... really bad. Even the other slavers couldn't stand him.

His conversion came very gradually. There seemed to be a number of 'false starts' when an apparent work of grace would take place in his heart, but then Newton would go back to his 'old ways'. Most of us would have written him off... but not Jesus Christ. The Lord Jesus had John Newton in His sights, and for Newton there would finally be no escaping God's 'Amazing Grace'.

Now what I find so encouraging about this is that his life was/is a real testimony of the dogged perseverance of the Lord in the saving of a wayward soul. Some... a few, a precious few... have a 'Damascus Road' experience whereby their conversion is so radical and complete that they seem never to really look back or wander away again. But for many of us, and for many of those for whom we are longing and praying, the road to final conversion seems much more twisted and tortuous. Some for whom we are praying and hoping seem to have one false beginning after another... a good season followed by yet another foray into the 'world'. The 'old ways' just seem to have such a grip on them. How many mothers are sighing out endless prayers for a wayward child? Who can count the tears of a father as he watches his dear child wander still farther into the darkness? How many spouses are longing and waiting for the conversion of an unbelieving partner? How many faithful friends are looking year in year out for God to do a saving work in the life of their companion?

If you have a wayward loved one or friend for whom you have been praying and longing for their soul's salvation, I want you to take great encouragement from the life of John Newton.

Some souls are hard to save! But God is able! Don't give up!
Keep on praying, hoping, believing.

Keep right on taking every God-given opportunity to share the Good News of Jesus Christ. Keep seeking to live a winsome life that the beauty of Christ may be seen even through you. Don't be discouraged by the false starts and relapses. God is able to conquer the toughest soul. In my (now many) years as a pastor, I have seen many 'John Newtons'... weary and wayward souls who seem to walk a good way with the Lord, and then... oh! Old habits and haunts come calling and... back to the darkness they go.

BUT God will have the last Word, and His grace is sufficient to open the most stubborn, lost and worldly hearts. He can make a trophy of Grace out of a tragic life. As long as there is a God of Grace ruling this Universe there is hope for the John Newtons of this world.

Keep praying,
Witnessing,
Believing.
DON'T GIVE UP!

Yours,

John Gillespie.

Notes:~

O God, thou art my God; early will I seek Thee:
my soul thirsteth for
Thee, my flesh longeth for Thee in a dry and thirsty land,
where no water is.
(Psalm 63:1)

As Rich In Christ As We Want To Be

Dear Beloved in Christ,

I want to take a few minutes to encourage you in the good and Godly habit of developing a daily quiet time with the Lord Jesus.

I realise that many of you have for many years been spending time with the Lord Jesus most every, if not every, day and have found the practice to be a life-line for your soul. May this offering of mine encourage you to continue on in your private time with the Lord.

But I am most concerned here to encourage and motivate those of us who have yet to establish a daily life-line with the Lord; to see the value in it and to acquire the basic skills needed to have a helpful quiet time every day.

1. The Value of a Daily Quiet Time:

I can put it this strongly: There is no substitute for a time each day with the Lord. Look at the verse at the top of this letter. Do you see the desperation in the Psalmist? He must meet with the Lord! He will rise early to spend time with his God. There is a thirst in his soul that only the Lord can satisfy. Personally, I cannot exist without a peaceful 'still point' with my Saviour every day. He is my Source and my Strength and I cannot do without time with Him.

I am praying that God will make us all desperate for Him. The Lord Jesus, God the Son, was desperate for time with His Heavenly Father. Want proof? Have a look:

And in the morning, [Jesus] rising up a great while before day, He went out, and departed into a solitary place, and there prayed.
(Mark 1:35)

Now, if the Lord Jesus needed a dedicated prayer time, what does that say about you and me?

2. Helpful Keys to a Successful Quiet Time:

What I am going to share now is not 'rocket science'... it is more important than that. But these keys are not difficult to grasp and they will help you.

Discipline your sleep habits (yes, I really mean this!).
If meeting with Jesus is important enough to you, then try going to bed early enough to allow you to rise early enough to give you time to meet with the Lord Jesus before the start of your busy day. Don't even try to burn the candle at both ends (the Bible warns that this is a vain practice (Psalm 127:2). Retire a bit earlier in the night because you have an appointment with the Maker of the Universe in the morning.

Truly believe that the Lord Himself will address you personally through His Word.

I believe that the Bible shows me Christ and reveals God's mind to me when I prayerfully read it. If you are not sure where to begin, I suggest a chapter of Mark's Gospel every morning, and a section of Psalm 119. When you read it, ask the Holy Spirit to illuminate it to you. Seek to discover a new facet of Jesus Christ, what He is like, and how He acts. See what insights you can gain into what it will mean for you to trust and follow Christ today.

Take a few minutes to pray over your day.
Bring your family to Christ in prayer. Pray for their protection from sin and Satan. Pray for your Church, pastor, Community Group. As you develop your 'muscles', your Quiet Time prayer list will undoubtedly grow.

Finally, take a few minutes and worship the Lord.
Thank Him for His grace. Reflect upon what you have learned in your Scripture reading. Deliberately open your heart to Him and ask Him to be your joy and strength for the day ahead.

The above may take only twenty minutes, especially at the start. But it can become a life-changing part of your day that will grow and develop in richness and depth.*

Well, I hope this helps you and encourages you to pursue a deeper walk with the Lord.

Be sure of this: We will be as rich in Christ as we want to be. Please don't fail to develop this in your life. May the Lord give us all a true hunger for Himself and the grace to seek a deeper relationship with Himself.

Yours,

John Gillespie.

* There are many helpful tools such as UCB notes, Daily Bread, Every Day With Jesus, that can help you kick-start or establish the good habit of a daily Quiet Time. Don't hesitate to try one if you feel it would be helpful. But you can also try the scheme I suggest above.

Notes:~

Love each other as I have loved you.
(John 15:12)

The Rocky Road Of Relationships

Dear Church,

Having been privileged to be a pastor now for more than a quarter of a century, I can confidently say that virtually all problems in church life fall into one of the following two categories:

1. Doctrinal Problems
2. Relational Problems

Here in the GCC Family we are, thankfully, free from most doctrinal problems... we tend to believe the right things.

But... we are not immune from relational problems.

Be sure of this: Satan can undo a Church as certainly through strife between brothers and sisters as he can through heresy. We have spent countless hours lamenting unforgiveness between brothers and sisters. We have cried rivers of tears over fractured relationships. God's work has often been brought to a grinding halt through misunderstanding, pride, hardness of heart towards another for whom Christ died, or via good old-fashioned, Satan-glorifying unforgiveness.

Getting along with one another is not an option for those of us in the Body of Christ. It is a direct command from Headquarters. Consider the following Scriptures:

Therefore, if you are offering your gift at the altar and there remember that your brother has something against you, leave your gift there in front of the altar. First go and be reconciled to your brother; then come and offer your gift.
(Matthew 5:23-24)

My command is this: Love each other as I have loved you.
(John 15:12)

See to it that no one misses the grace of God and that no bitter root grows up to cause trouble and defile many.
(Hebrews 12:15)

I could multiply Bible passages, filling pages on this most vital theme. You can discover them for yourself. The point is obvious and unavoidable: The Body of Christ travels on a Road of Relationships. We cannot fail to 'seek peace and pursue it' (1 Peter 3:11).

When relationships are undervalued, or allowed to collapse, the entire journey of the Church is jeopardized. It is no use saying 'it's the other guy's fault'. God calls each of us to be 'peacemakers'. It is no use excusing the rift as a mere 'private matter' between 'private parties'. In a Body there are no private matters. When we let the sun go down on our anger, we give the Devil a foothold (Ephesians 4:27). When we work hard for good relationships and forgive quickly, we give Satan little room to work.

I have very little fear that the Evil One will get into our midst through heresy from our pulpits or Community Groups. Our teaching is pretty sound.

But...

Let us not be so foolish as to think he will not try another tactic to side-track this great work! Let's not even give him a chance!
When we fail to honour one another
serve one another
love one another
forgive one another
seek out fellowship with one another
repent to one another
cherish one another

... we do the Devil's work... just as certainly as if I or another stands in the pulpit and proclaims heresy.

Now... let's make it positive:

When we honour one another
serve one another
love one another
forgive one another
seek out fellowship with one another
repent to one another
cherish one another

85

... we do Christ's work... just as certainly as if I or another stands in the pulpit and proclaims God's glorious Truth.

Finally, before I close read below the wonderful words of Psalm 133. The blessings of unity are plain to see.

> Behold, how good and how pleasant it is for brethren
> to dwell together in unity!
> It is like the precious ointment upon the head,
> that ran down upon the beard,
> even Aaron's beard: that went down to
> the skirts of his garments;
> As the dew of Hermon, and as the dew
> that descended upon the mountains of Zion:
> for there the LORD commanded the blessing,
> even life for evermore.

Let the words sink in... and determine to live in harmony with your brothers and sisters.

Grace and Peace to all of you,

John Gillespie.

Notes:~

The Gospel is the Power of God...
(Romans 1:16)

The Confidence Question

Dear Friends,

Well, I confess that I am excited.

I am confident in Jesus Christ and His Gospel. I believe that when He said:

'I will build My Church and the gates of hell will not prevail against it' that He meant it.

I know that we are in 'recession'... but the Gospel has never had a problem flourishing in poor times and places.

I know that we are in a 'post-Christian' society... but the Gospel was made for hard ground... it does well in dry soil.

I understand (after living here for twenty-two years) that thing called 'British Reserve'... but I believe it to be no match for a Message that finds expression in any culture, from Africa to the Arctic.

Jesus Christ is Lord
and that settles the confidence question.

So, I want to pass this spirit of being encouraged on to you, especially as far as evangelism goes.

First, be aware and convinced that by far the most effective form of evangelism is personal witnessing via relationships. Yes, we can have programmes and strategies, and at times we should, but *most people* (86% according to studies) *come to Christ by personal contacts*.

So, my first job as your pastor will always be to offer Christ to you from the Scriptures, so that you might be made strong to witness for Him in your world.

Next, following our time in Revelation I will begin a walk through the Gospel of Mark. Mark's Gospel is essentially an evangelistic tract. It is made for unbelievers. It is fast-paced and presents Jesus Christ as the Son of God and the sinner's Hope.

Throughout this whole time I will be asking, hoping and expecting that we will be praying regularly for the Holy Spirit to awaken faith in Christ amongst our friends and neighbours.

God is faithful, and I believe that He will Glorify His Son through the salvation of many as we put our confidence in Him.

Please join with me in being expectant and prayerful.

> Enlarge, Inflame, and Fill my heart;
> With boundless Charity Divine
> So shall I all my strength exert
> And love them with a love like Thine
> And lead them to thy Wounded Side,
> The Sheep, for Whom their Shepherd Died!

Yours for the Gospel,

John Gillespie.

Notes:~

Very early in the morning, while it was still dark, Jesus got up, left the house and went off to a solitary place, where He prayed. Simon and his companions went to look for Him, and when they found Him, they exclaimed: 'Everyone is looking for you!'

Jesus replied: 'Let us go somewhere else - to the nearby villages - so I can preach there also. That is why I have come.' So He travelled throughout Galilee, preaching in their synagogues and driving out demons.
(Mark 1:35-39)

The Tyranny Of The Urgent

Dear Church Family,

The above scene from the life of the Lord Jesus is packed with lessons for those of us living in these busy times.

Mark's Gospel is a *busy* Gospel. Jesus is on the go. He moves quickly. His days are packed with ministry. People are pressing in. There is an urgency about His movements. He is on a mission.

But...

...He takes time...

...He takes T I M E...

to Pray

Look at the above passage with me. We are allowed to peek at The Lord of the Universe having His 'quiet time'. Notice a few things:

He *rises early*. He conquers His own spirit and the cosy call of the mattress to set about this all-important business of being *with His Father.*

He *finds a quiet place*. He will have the whole day with others... He needs *alone time* with His Father.

He *prays*. He is checking in with Headquarters. He is getting His priorities set for the day.

Now, notice what happens: His precious quiet time with His Father... *gets interrupted!* (Has that ever happened to you?)

...'Everyone is looking for you!...

This is called 'the tyranny of the urgent'. It frantically begs us to leave off what we are doing and to follow *its* agenda for us... NOW!

But, the Lord Jesus is *not subject* to the tyrant! He has spent time with the Father, and is free to do what is *important*, not what is *urgent*.

Jesus actually says 'No' to the urgent: 'Let's go someplace else.'

That is Freedom!
That is Power!
That is being 'Spirit Led'!

Busy People! Hear this: **Prayer saves time.** It lines our priorities up with God's and delivers us from the tyranny of the urgent. It empowers us to say 'no' to the agenda of man and 'yes' to the call of the Lord.

As individuals, as families, and as a church, we need to hear from the Lord. *His* burden is easy compared with that of the urgent. But we cannot hear from Him unless we take time to be with Him. We need, as a priority, to get before the Lord. *We need quiet, prayerful TIME* with God. If the Lord Jesus did, then all of us do.

I encourage you, busy friend, to make a wonderful habit of daily time with Jesus. Believe me, it will *save* you more time than it takes, and *deliver* you from the tyranny of the urgent.

Grace and peace be yours in abundance through our Lord and Saviour Jesus Christ.

Yours,

John Gillespie.

Notes:~

*Very early in the morning, while it was still dark, Jesus got up,
left the house and went off to a solitary place, where He prayed.
Simon and his companions went to look for Him, and when they
found Him, they exclaimed: 'Everyone is looking for you!'*

*Jesus replied: 'Let us go somewhere else — to the nearby
villages — so I can preach there also. That is why I have come.'
So He travelled throughout Galilee, preaching in their
synagogues and driving out demons.*
(Mark 1:35-39)

To Walk In Freedom

Dear Friends,

Let's look again at the Lord Jesus at prayer and discover the
transforming truth that His prayer life actually delivered Him from
the 'Tyranny of the Urgent' and enabled Him to walk in the will of
His Heavenly Father. This is to walk in freedom.

Let's let Mark's Gospel set the scene for us one again:
*Very early in the morning, while it was still dark, Jesus got up,
left the house and went off to a solitary place, where He prayed.
Simon and his companions went to look for Him, and when they
found Him, they exclaimed: 'Everyone is looking for you!'*

*Jesus replied: 'Let us go somewhere else — to the nearby
villages — so I can preach there also. That is why I have come.'
So He travelled throughout Galilee, preaching in their
synagogues and driving out demons. (Mark 1:35-39)*

Remember what we discovered last week: Because Jesus sought His
Father's will *He was able to say 'NO!' to the urgent demand of
Peter;* 'Everyone is looking for you!' The implication of the scene is
plain:

**Because Jesus set aside time to be with His Father,
He saved time.**
He was able to spend His day doing the *important* not the *urgent*.

The application for us, both as individuals and as a
Church Family is clear:

God has a purpose for us that He wants us to walk in:
For we are God's workmanship, created in Christ Jesus to
do good works, which God prepared in advance for us to do.
(Ephesians 2:10)

God does not *want* us to do everything! He wants us to do
certain things. He wants us to say 'yes' to His agenda, and 'no'
to ours, or others' for us. But, we cannot discover His will for
us, and freely walk in it if we do not seek Him. We are called
first and foremost to be attentive to the Lord; to be People of
the Spirit; to be seeking His heart for this work.

We are not called just to be busy!

Over the years, I and others have gathered hundreds of times
to pray and ask the Lord to take us where He wants us to go as
a Church Family. Countless others of you have met in the
'secret place' of your prayer 'closet' to ask God's favour and
leading to be upon us. As a result *God, not man, has shaped
this Church*. He has guided and directed us to be where we
are, who we are, what we are.

But the 'Tyranny of the Urgent' does not leave us easily! The
Tyrant knocks on our door and demands that we be a busy
Church, a noisy bunch, a driven people!

If we leave off prayer, if we simply 'react', if we mistake
human sweat for the Spirit's power, we will simply exhaust
ourselves, and miss God's better call upon our lives. If we
allow 'strategy meetings' to replace prayer meetings, we will
have become a carnal Church: men of flesh, and not of the
Spirit; subjects of the Tyrant.

God can and will lead as the People of God seek Him. When we
spend time with God and receive His dreams and visions, we
are delivered from the Tyranny of the Urgent, and freed to do
the things that the Lord has ordained for us to do!

Beloved, the key is seeking the Lord, being a praying People,
desiring to be a Spirit-led People.

May the Lord Jesus free us to follow Him.

Yours,

John Gillespie.

Notes: ~

*He giveth power to the faint; and to them
that have no might He increases their strength.
(Isaiah 40:29)*

See You At The Finish Line

Dear Church,

I want to tell you a true story of the power of the Word of God and faith in a real life situation.

I want to tell you the story of Glenn Cunningham.

Glenn Cunningham was born on a farm in Kansas in 1909. He and his older brother Floyd attended a little one room country schoolhouse together. The two brothers had the job of lighting the pot-bellied stove early on winter mornings in order to have the school warm and welcoming for the rest of their classmates upon arrival.

One cold morning, when Glenn was eight and Floyd was ten, they arrived as usual to light the stove. They normally put kerosene (paraffin) on the wood to light it. On this fateful morning, someone had mistakenly left a gasoline (petrol) can in the place of the kerosene can for the boys to use.

You can guess what happened...

There were still a few hot embers in the stove. The moment the petrol touched those coals the petrol exploded. Glenn was blown clear out of the building. His brother was left inside. Bravely, the little eight-year-old re-entered the fiery schoolroom to try to drag his big brother to safety.

Floyd perished in the fire.

Glenn was horribly burned... especially on his legs. *He had lost all the flesh on his knees and shins and all the toes on his left foot. Also, his transverse arch was practically destroyed**. The country doctor saw no hope for little Glenn's legs. He asked permission of the parents to amputate.

But Glenn had praying parents.

God gave a very precious Word from the Bible to Glenn's mother, which she took as a promise for Glenn:

He giveth power to the faint; and to them that have no might He increases their strength.

Even the youths shall faint and be weary,
and the young men shall utterly fall:
But they that wait upon the LORD shall renew their strength;
they shall mount up with wings as eagles;
**they shall run, and not be weary; and they shall walk,
and not faint.**
(Isaiah 40:29-31)

With this promise in her heart, she refused the good doctor's advice, believing that the Lord had a greater purpose in this tragedy.

There and then began months and years of faith-filled 'rehab'... farm-style. Glenn's parents patiently, persistently and prayerfully began to massage his little legs. Standing (literally) on the promise God had given them, Glenn began to walk about the farmyard... on sticks at first. It was hard work.
Nothing came easy...

Time passed... and Glenn ran for the US Olympic Team in 1932 and 1936. He set the world record for the mile and the world indoor record for the 1500 meters. The man who became known as 'The Kansas Flyer' was declared in 1933 to be his nation's top athlete and many to this day consider Glenn Cunningham to be the finest distance runner his country ever produced.

Now, *not every story has such an ending*. But...!... The lessons of Glenn's story are for us all:

There is power in knowing the Word of God (we cannot 'stand upon' promises that we have never even read).

The Holy Spirit can 'quicken' faith in those who are willing to stand upon the promises of God and not simply give up.

*There are victories to be fought for and won
through faith and prayer.*

Nothing of value comes easy... and there is no glory for the spiritually lazy.

A promise, received, believed and acted upon can decide the destiny of a life, a family, a nation... an eternity.

Brothers and Sisters, how many victories are we missing because we aren't engaging in the Fight of Faith? How many opportunities to live for the Glory of God are being passed by because it is easier to watch TV than to watch and pray?

Let's be people of radical and costly faith. Let's say 'no' to unbelief. Let's set a course where either 1: God comes through or 2: we fail. Let's get *into* the Word and then *go out to* the World... Let's do the hard things.

See you at the finish line,

John Gillespie.

(*Wikipedia)

Notes:~

...for God loves a cheerful giver...
(2 Corinthians 9:7)

Let's Talk Money

Dear Brothers and Sisters,

I have been asked by those in our church family who deal with finance to share with you something of God's heart from the Scriptures concerning our stewardship of our money, and in particular, addressing the question:

'What does it mean to honour God through giving
to our local Church?'

Now, for a pastor to have a 'money talk' with his congregation can be sort of in the same league as a father having a 'sex talk' with his teenager. I am not suggesting that you are adolescent, but rather, that it may be that we both get a little bit nervous and that neither of us *really* wants to do this...

But here let's lift our game a bit and bring this discussion out of the league of 'I really don't want to talk about this but...' to 'Let me really share God's heart (and mine) with you about this heart issue...'

Let's pretend we are sitting on the sofa together chatting over a cup of coffee.

Beloved, this is a *heart issue*. That is why the Lord Jesus spoke of it so often. How we view money, and how we use money, and how we give our money, and how we spend our money, says more about our hearts than any other area of our lives, apart from how we treat others (the two are intertwined).

There is a great scripture passage tucked away in the middle of Paul's second letter to the Corinthians, which tells us enough for our time together today; not everything on the subject... but it gives us a good place from which to start:

Remember this: Whoever sows sparingly will also reap sparingly,
and whoever sows generously will also reap generously.
Each man should give what he has decided in his heart to give, not
reluctantly or under compulsion, for God loves a cheerful giver.

And God is able to make all grace abound to you, so that in all things at all times, having all that you need, you will abound in every good work.

Read it... ponder it for a few minutes. Its message is so plain that there is really little I have, or need, to add, so let me just set the scene (read it for yourself in 2 Corinthians 9:6+7):

There was a financial recession in Jerusalem and the Church there was in a bad way money-wise;
Paul was asking the Church in Greece to help out;
The poorer churches in Macedonia had already given generously, even out of their poverty;
Paul had asked the comparatively rich Christians to give as well, and they promised to do so;
Now Paul is sending a friend called Titus and two others to them to actually collect their offering...
it is time for the Corinthians to 'make good' on their promise;
Paul was worried that they would not come through and so writes to encourage them.

Jump your eyes back to the Bible passage. Notice a few obvious truths...

1. You get out what you put in: Sow a little, reap a little; sow a lot, reap a lot (this is a principle so obvious that we now term it a 'no-brainer'... you don't even have to *think* to understand it).

*This means that giving should be **generous** (not miserly)*

2. When it comes to giving, it is not about having your arm twisted or being guilt-tripped into coughing up... it is about deciding in your heart what *God* would have you give.

*This means that giving should be **deliberate** (not haphazard)*

3. God loves it when we give in a spirit of Joy, not in a begrudging manner. God can do a lot with a little when there is a joyful, worshipping heart within the giver and behind the gift.

*This means that giving should be a **joyful act of worship** (not just a duty)*

4. God is able to multiply grace to us so that we can be even more generous, at all times, in all ways, for all things.

*This means that giving is **faith-led** (not fear-driven)*

Well, my cup of coffee is about empty... but our 'money' talk is not over(!) Please ponder what I have shared so far... go to the Lord with it and bring your own heart to the Lord over this...

I'll be back next week for another heart-to-heart.

Put the kettle on,

John Gillespie.

Notes:~

For where your treasure is, there your heart will be also.
(Matthew 6:21)

Let's Talk Money Some More

Dear Church,

I hope you have kept the kettle on, as it is time for the rest of our 'heart-to-heart' about giving. Hopefully we are over our nervousness by now and realise that we are sharing together about an issue that belongs in the very centre of our Christian living, not somewhere along the perimeter.

Financial stewardship is not a side issue...

...It is an issue that reveals much about our hearts, and where in fact our treasure is.

Jesus put it this way:

For where your **treasure** is, there your **heart** will be also.
(Matthew 6:21)

Our hearts follow our *treasure*. Generous, Deliberate, Joyful, Faith-led giving *leads our hearts* in devotion to the Lord Jesus.

When I sit at my kitchen table and pay my bills and balance my cheque-book (something I am sure you do too) I consecrate my heart to the Lord as I figure in my tithe. Giving orients my heart aright. It is a deliberate way of me saying, 'Lord Jesus, I really do aim to treasure You above everything else.'

Consider this: There is a remarkable order in our going to Heaven. We go in four stages.

First: Our Treasure goes (that needs to happen *Now*)
Second: Our hearts go (this follows as a matter of course)
Third: Our souls go (this will happen the moment we die)
Finally: Our bodies go (at the Resurrection of the dead)

Many are hoping for the third and fourth without paying heed to the first and second! We want to treasure earthly things above all, and have our hearts thrilled with things below... and then, 'presto!', suddenly treasure Christ supremely the moment we die and have to leave our earthly playthings behind!

Your stewardship *today* will do as much to direct your heart heavenward as will anything else.

Let's pour one more cup of coffee before I go...

We looked last week at the four keys to giving in 2 Corinthians 9.

Just by way of reminder (and with no apologies for repeating such an important list of principles):

> 1. You get out what you put in: Sow a little, reap a little; sow a lot, reap a lot.

*This means that giving should be **generous** (not miserly)*

> 2. When it comes to giving, it is not about having your arm twisted or being guilt-tripped into coughing up... it is about deciding in your heart what *God* would have you give.

*This means that giving should be **deliberate** (not haphazard)*

> 3. God loves it when we give in a spirit of Joy, not in a begrudging manner. God can do a lot with a little when there is a joyful, worshipping heart within the giver and behind the gift.

*This means that giving should be a **joyful act of worship** (not just a duty)*

> 4. God is able to multiply grace to us so that we can be even more generous, at all times, in all ways, for all things.

*This means that giving is **faith-led** (not fear-driven)*

I just want to add a fifth key principle from another passage in 1 Corinthians 16:1,2:

> Now about the collection for God's people:
> Do what I told the Galatian churches to do.
> On the first day of every week,
> each one of you should set aside a sum of money
> in keeping with his income...

Here the Apostle is instructing the Corinthians to do what he had instructed the Galatians to do (so, we can assume that he would instruct us, wherever we reside, to do the same!). He instructs them to *regularly* give:

On the first day of every week, each one of you should set aside a sum of money in keeping with his income...

Churches *need* regular giving. We need regular giving if we are to set our budgets, support our missionaries, and develop our ministries.

So, we see in these passages the five key principles to Godly giving: Generous, Deliberate, Joyful, Faith-led, Regular.

Well, our time is about up... coffee is all but finished.

Before I leave, I earnestly want to impress upon you the need for us to take this matter most seriously.

Your Soul needs you to be a good steward of your finances; God's Kingdom needs you to be a good steward of your finances.

Christ alone is worthy of being our supreme treasure, and our care over earthly treasures will lead our hearts to treasure Him supremely.

Yours,

John Gillespie.

Notes:~

Week 34

Remember your leaders, who spoke the Word of God to you.
(Hebrews 13:7)

The Glory Of Our Faith

Beloved,

This week I want to talk about someone who was born around five hundred years ago, but I will only tell you his name if you promise, please, not to screw up your face and close the book... promise to hear me out first.

Promise?

I want to talk about John Calvin.

Now, hang in there for a moment or two. Don't do the classic default: 'Calvin! Wasn't he that *Predestination* dude?' 'Wasn't he some *sour preacher* from the Middle Ages?' 'Didn't he *burn* some guy at the stake?'

I think it is worth remembering a man who is, to this very day...

the most widely read Christian author outside of the New Testament writers.

Let's leave our prejudices aside for a few moments. John Calvin was pre-eminently a *God-centred* man who longed to restore *God-centredness* to the Church.

He was for decades a gentle, shy and faithful pastor in Geneva. He was faithful to his wife, Idelette, whom he adored and buried. He fought battles for Truth in a cruel and rough age, and his pain-racked body did not see out its fifty-fifth year.

John Calvin had one great concern in his life: the restoration of True Worship to the Church. Consumed with the majesty of the God of the Bible, his holy heart was broken by the idolatry, coldness and worldliness of the Church in his age. Radically converted out of the superstitions of medieval Catholicism in 1533, he immersed himself in the wonders of the Gospel. It is a mistake to think that his life was all about 'predestination'. Yes, he saw the doctrine in the Bible, so he believed it and defended it. But it was not his 'party piece'. (Indeed, his Geneva Catechism did not even mention it.)

The great doctrine that gripped him, the Truth upon which he was convinced that the true worship of a Holy God depended, was none other than that of Justification by Grace through Faith. Calvin saw (rightly) that this was the Truth upon which the door to true worship was hinged.

Let me explain what he saw... because I believe we need to see it too:

The doctrine of Justification by Grace through Faith is unique to the Bible.
No other religion has anything remotely like it, and it is the glory of the Christian faith.

It tells us of the unmerited favour of God given to undeserving sinners through the death of Christ. It tells us of the transference of our sin, guilt and pollution to a crucified Saviour, and of His righteousness being transferred to us by the gracious decree of God. It delivers the sin-sick soul from striving to appease an angry 'god' and sets the Church free to worship the Living God aright.

This is the doctrine upon which the Christian Church rises or falls. This Truth is the only hope for the human race, and the clear channel for promoting the Glory of God.

Now, believe it or not, for centuries down to Calvin's day, most of the Church was ignorant of this glorious truth. Bibles were unread... even by the clergy. People lived in the darkness of religious superstition. *God could not be truly worshipped because the wonders of His saving love were not known*. It was down to a brave bunch of men (and women too) with names like Huss, Luther, Knox, Farel, Zwingli, Tyndale and Wycliffe, to open their Bibles and preach the Gospel against the rage of the medieval Church who saw such men as threats to their power.

Beloved, we too today can forget the wonders of the Gospel of Justification by Grace through Faith. We can easily default into performance-based 'churchianity'... joyless, superstitious, man-centred and dead.

Worship is what the Church exists for. But it must be *true worship*. Not just any type will do, be it ever so sincere or exhilarating. It must spring from a heart resting and rejoicing in the Gospel, or it is not Christian, and therefore odious to the True God. That is what the God-saturated John Calvin saw and spent his life seeking to restore the Church to.

We do well today to remember this great man still, some five hundred years after his birth, to thank God for a true minister of the Gospel, and the fertile soil of Truth that he ploughed and in which the Church could worship and grow.

May The Lord raise up such men today.

Yours for Christ's glory,

John Gillespie.

Notes:~

Week 35

I have hidden your Word in my heart,
that I might not sin against you...
(Psalm 119:11)

Hide The Word In Your Heart

Dear Church,

How many verses can you recall from reading your Bible during the last week?

Give it a try...

Try harder... HARDER... *HARDER...*

Tough, isn't it? But, let me assure you that it is worth the effort.

There are at least three great reasons to commit the Word of God to memory.

1. There is *great power over sin and temptation* in the Word of God memorised:

The Psalmist put it this way:
'I have hidden your Word in my heart, that I might not sin
Against you...' (Psalm 119:11)

Every true child of God struggles with indwelling sin. Indeed, of all his struggles, this is the greatest. The Truth of God, His Word, hidden in one's heart (memorised) drives out indwelling sin, renews one's affections, and empowers one to battle valiantly against sin and temptation.

2. There is *great strength for the weary soul* in the Word of God memorised:

Again, the Psalmist said:
'My soul is weary with sorrow. Strengthen me according to
Thy Word.' (Psalm 119:28)

Every true child of God battles with discouragement and sorrow of soul. God's Word indwelling in the heart strengthens one against weariness of soul. The Word memorised can be speedily recalled and applied to the burdened, joyless heart, driving away sorrow and bathing the soul in light.

3. There is *much wisdom and deliverance from folly* in God's Word memorised:

Our Psalmist wrote:
'Your commands make me wiser than my enemies, for they are Ever with me.' (Psalm 119:98)

Every true child of God contends with enemies. Satan himself, the enemy, taunts the believer. God's Word is 'ever with' the disciple who commits it to memory. It is there when needed to give wisdom and insight beyond the natural. The Christian with the Word of God in his heart is wise and therefore not easy prey for the enemy of his soul.

Friend, this is serious. The cause of Christ, the very Glory of God and the salvation of sinners depends, at least in some part, upon the health of *our* souls. The well-being of our families and church is directly linked to the strength of *our* inner selves. Committing the Word of God to our hearts is vital to the overall well-being of not only *our* souls, but the very cause of Christ.

As I have said many times before, you are as Godly, as spiritually whole, as you want to be. Dwelling upon the Word of God and allowing it to dwell within you will do as much good for your life — and the lives around you — as anything I know.

Here are a few of the Scripture passages that my wife Tessa, our kids and I have committed to memory. If you have not memorised passages before, give these a try...

Isaiah 53

Philippians 2:1-11
John 15:1-17

Galatians 6:7-10
Psalm 91

Colossians 3:12-17

Matthew 5:1-20
Psalm 1
John 1:1-18

Romans 8:28-39

See what you can memorise from the Bible between this week and next.

Go on, stir up the old grey cells and see what happens!
Yours,

John Gillespie.

Notes:~

Week 36

Oh, that you would bless me and enlarge my territory!
(1 Chronicles 4:10)

The Man Who Asked For More

Dear Saints,

I am not satisfied. Well, I am and I am not.

I rejoice with a satisfied soul in the finished work of Jesus Christ for me in the Cross.

My life is rich in the things of God. I have more than I need and more than I deserve.

The Church I am a member of is a remarkable Church in so many ways...
There is much to be thankful for and satisfied in.

But... I WANT MORE. I want more purpose and influence for me, for my family and for my church. I want a deeper appreciation of the mission that is before us. I want more heart for the Gospel and for the lost. I want to be a part of a greater work, a costlier work, for God's Glory.

Currently, my family and I are reading through Bruce Wilkinson's amazing little book *The Prayer of Jabez*. Although I've read the book before, the powerful prayer of that ancient man is affecting and inspiring me again.

Here it is:

'Jabez was more honourable than his brothers. His mother named him Jabez saying, "I gave birth to him in pain." Jabez cried out to the God in Israel. "Oh, that you would bless me and enlarge my territory! Let your hand be with me and keep me from harm so that I will be free from pain."
And God granted his request.'
(1 Chronicles 4:9,10)

109

Now, there are many great principles in that brief biography, and I commend Bruce Wilkinson's little book to you to help you discover them. But I just want to focus on the fact that this man Jabez could have been content with who he was, and his lot in life, but *he was not*. He actually asked God for *more*. 'Lord! Enlarge my territory!' 'Bless me!' 'Put your hand upon me!' And then we have the epilogue to his biography: 'And God granted his request.'

I want to dare us to pray like Jabez prayed. Putting his heart-felt prayer into a frame for us today, can we dare to pray for richer lives in Christ, for more effective ministries (whatever yours may be), for more God-given opportunities to live for Him, to witness for Him, to serve others in His Name?

Most of us want easier lives. Like water, we seek the paths of least resistance. How about seeking after *effective* lives, regardless of whether they be easy or not? Bruce Wilkinson puts it like this:

'...when we are deciding what size of territory [life effectiveness] God has in mind for us, we keep an equation in our hearts that adds up something like this:

My abilities + experience + training + my personality and experience
+
my past + the expectation of others
= **My assigned territory**

God's [equation for us] would look more like this:

My willingness and weakness + God's will and supernatural power
= **My expanding territory**'

The key is putting *The Lord* in the equation! We leave the Lord of all provision and power out of our figuring and then settle too quickly for lives of 'quiet desperation'. We believe too little, and therefore ask for too little.

I am praying for a divine *dis*satisfaction that will drive us to pound on Heaven's door and dare to ask for MORE... Not more *busyness*, but *effectiveness*.

I am praying that as a people we live in the place where *if God does not come through... then we have had it*. I am longing that our territory (range of effectiveness for Christ) be determined *not* by our natural means and abilities, but by the *faithfulness and call of God*.

I am praying that Church becomes a dangerous place, where God turns up often and expands our boundaries.

I am praying for more effective, focused, harder ministries... For dreams and visions that exceed our natural grasp, but which are possible in Christ's power.

I am not satisfied... yet...

Are you?

Grace, peace and divine *DIS*satisfaction be yours in Christ Jesus Our Lord,

John Gillespie.

Notes:~

Take My yoke upon you, and learn of Me
(Jesus in Matthew 11:29)

A Personal Invitation

Friends,

Jesus Christ invites us to *Himself*. He does not invite us to a religion. He invites us to a relationship. 'Learn of ME,' He says. Let us consider the wonders of this invitation together.

First, *Who* is it that is giving this invitation; 'Learn of ME'? Well, it is none other than the Eternal God in human flesh. This is the one who created all that there is, for whom, in whom, and by whom *all things* exist and are sustained.

Imagine a great figure of society, perhaps the Queen herself, inviting *us*, *YOU*, to a deep knowledge of herself. 'I want you to be intimately acquainted with me. I want to bring you to my side and reveal my heart to your heart. I want to reveal my secrets to you. Come to me, and learn of me.'

Imagine a great musician, artist, poet, athlete, or scientist inviting *you* to *himself*... 'Learn of me!'

But no, this is the King of Kings. This is the One in whom are hidden 'all the treasures of wisdom and knowledge (Colossians 2:3). This One is 'fairer than ten thousand.' This One is:

> The Bread of Life
> The Rose of Sharon
> The Prince of Peace
> The Bright Morning Star
> The Shepherd of Our Souls

Are you 'Learning of Him?'

Second, for *whom* is the invitation? Hear it: 'Come unto Me *all* who are weary and heavy laden.' I am in that 'all', and so are you. This invitation is as broad as is the weary human race.

Take it personally, because it is given personally.

Next, for *what* are we being invited? A job list? A duty? No, we are being invited, warmly invited, to 'learn', 'discover', 'explore' Jesus Christ. This will require time. It will mean laying some other lesser things aside. It will mean a new agenda, new priorities. This journey of discovery will cost us, but it will be worth it, for He is:

> The Treasure hidden in a field,
> and The Pearl of Great Price.

More, the discovery will reach into Eternity, for this is the One Who embraces the ages, and in Whom are Eternal Pleasures.

Are you 'Learning of Him'?

Brothers and Sisters, we are called to be Jesus People. Whatever else we are, we need to be preeminently *His*.

The work of the Kingdom flows from a *relationship* with the King. The Church is not a secular business and its pastors are not managing directors. The Church is a living Body, a loving Bride, a learning Band of Followers. We flourish or fail as we are learning of, or ignoring, our Lord and Saviour.

To be powerful in public we need to be with Jesus in private.

To challenge our culture we need to cultivate our relationship with our Champion.

Apart from Christ we can do nothing. I want to live a Jesus-centred life, and I want to be a part of a Jesus-centred People. If we are 'learning of Him' we will impact our world. *He* will set the agenda. *He* will lead us. We will be spiritual people doing a spiritual work. It will be miraculous, and Jesus Christ *alone* will get all the credit.

Are you 'Learning of Him'?

Yours,

John Gillespie.

Notes:~

Come and have breakfast.
(John 21:12)

Hallowing The Ordinary

Dear Family,

Let me ask you a question. I want you to think real hard about this one...

What, for you, are the most remarkable occurrences in the Earthly life of our Lord Jesus? If I asked you to rank them, one to ten, what would be at the top? His Virgin Birth? The Feeding of the Five Thousand? His Atoning Death? What about His Resurrection in Power? I expect Raising Lazarus would make most of your lists, and probably mine too.

Most of us would have lists very similar to each others'. But! I think that I would have one *particular* event in the life of the Lord Jesus that many, most, (all?) of you would leave off. I am not saying that it would be at the *top* of my list, but I kid you not that it would make it into the top ten.

If I asked you to guess it, I don't think you would. Give it a try...

'Walking on water?' That's a great one, but... Nope
'Changing water into wine?' Nice try... No
'Riding into Jerusalem on a donkey?' Maybe the top twenty-five
'Cleansing the Temple with a whip?' Very cool, but...

Here's one that makes my *'Top Ten' Amazing Things That Jesus Did* list:

Let me set the scene: Jesus has risen from the dead (that *is* on my list), His disciples have gone out fishing. Jesus, the Risen One (The Lord of all the Universe) goes out to find them, calling to them from the shore. Peter sees Him, and swims to shore, the others following in the boat. John picks up the scene in chapter 21, verse 9, of his Gospel:

When they landed, they saw a fire of burning coals with some fish on it... Jesus said to them 'come and have breakfast'... Jesus came, took bread and gave it to them, and did the same with the fish. Alright, some of you think I have finally lost it, but just hang in there with me for a paragraph or two. This is the RISEN LORD here. He is in His GLORIFIED BODY. He has CONQUERED SIN AND DEATH. He now RULES UNCHALLENGED OVER SATAN...

And He...

Makes breakfast.

He *Makes Breakfast.*

I love this because it is so *un*spiritual! And in being *un*spiritual it tells us a truckload about...

...Ultimate Reality...

In making breakfast, Jesus, the risen Jesus, is Hallowing the ordinary. He is making a statement about Stuff. He is saying that the Kingdom of God is not just a wispy spiritual realm, but a solid place where matter matters and glorified people *eat food.*

Think about this! If we were inventing stories about Jesus, we would never have thought of the Risen Lord cooking breakfast. Floating maybe, having x-ray vision perhaps. But building a fire and serving a meal? Never! How awesome (right use of the word)! Awesome because it is so... ordinary.

Ultimate reality will be *solid,* not flimsy. 'Spiritual' does not mean vaporous. God is going to *redeem* Creation, not give up on it. He is going to resurrect *bodies,* not ghosts. We will live on a *renewed earth* not on puffy clouds.

This event is one of the most significant of our Lord Jesus' life and ministry because it tells us so much about Real Life. If in our glorified bodies stuff will matter, than so it should *now.* I fear that sometimes we try to be more spiritual than God designed us to be. If a Resurrected Lord makes breakfast, then it must be a good thing to rejoice in the ordinary *before* the Resurrection as well as after it. True, we are called to 'crucify our sinful natures', but that does not mean that sleeping on a bed of nails is holier than a thankful heart under a warm duvet on a winter's night. True, we are not to be 'mastered by anything', but that does not mean that we cannot receive all good things *now* in thankful anticipation of *then.* God gave us taste buds for a reason, and they will only get better, not be obliterated, in glory.

Prayer is Holy...
    But so is going to work
Bible reading is Godly...
    But so is good conversation

Witnessing honours God...
    But so does wrestling with your kids

Singing Praises is a blessing...
    But so is breakfast

Want to amend your list?

Yours,

John Gillespie.

Notes:~

Week 39

But you will receive power when the Holy Spirit comes upon you,
and you shall be My witnesses.
(Acts 1:8)

It's Not Just About Africa

Dear Church Family,

Our latest letter from Thailand* makes for thrilling reading and reminds us just why we are a mission-minded Church family. I want to add a portion of a personal letter sent from Bob and Dee Molton in West Africa to Tessa and myself. Don't rush over it, but take time to marvel with me at what God is doing through them:

We are very excited really at how God is blessing the
work here. God is doing amazing things in West Africa.
We believe this is a harvest time. We are so thrilled to
see people coming to the Lord regularly in almost all
the ministries represented by our families here at
school. On Sunday we will travel two hours to watch
about twelve people get baptised, from a collection
of villages where about twenty people were baptised
only a few months ago. God has been moving powerfully
through healing of the most dramatic sort; one man was
dying of Aids — was literally on his death bed — got up
off his bed and walked! He is now the proud father of a
new baby son and his wife has also come to the Lord.
Another old sorcerer — more than eighty years old —
has given the rest of his life to Jesus and was baptised
last time. I look forward to meeting him. We have a
waiting list of nineteen kids. God is sending labourers
into the harvest. We've started a building project to
help us accommodate these new families. Now the
school serves twenty different mission agencies and that
in itself is fabulous. Also seventeen nationalities — pray
for us that Jesus will always be our unity — giving us
the grace and wisdom we need.
Loads of love, Dee.

Stories like these could be multiplied many times in the lives of people sent out from this Church. We need to rejoice in these great works of God and praise God for allowing us to be partners in such great works through our giving, sending, going and praying.

BUT! Let's all remember our definition of Mission:

117

Mission is the purposeful crossing of boundaries of unbelief with the Gospel of Jesus Christ.

This means that mission is not just to happen in Thailand or West Africa. It means that it can and must happen right here... through *us*. Of course God is filling those who have been sent to far-flung lands with His Holy Spirit so that they can be Christ's witnesses... But do we realise that He is ready and waiting and willing to do the same with us... right here?

Brother, Sister, let's not leave it to Africa. I don't want to just read about what God is doing in the Far East. I want our own stories to be written right here, where we are, God working through us to bring glory to His Name and blessing to a lost and hurting world *right here*.

Get on your knees and *ask* God to fill *you*. See His anointing of power on *your* life. Ask Him to help you love the person next door (do you even know their name?). Discover what boundaries of unbelief exist right around you. Pray for courage to cross them.

Wherever you live the world is at your doorstep; the Mission field is all around us. The Gospel is still, and always will be, the only answer to the cries of the human heart... and we have it.

Let's believe for some great stories to be written right here... through us.

Grace to all through our Lord Jesus Christ,

John Gillespie.

(*Grace Community Church has sent out many missionaries to all parts of the world and supports them prayerfully and financially in their ministries.)

Notes:~

Simon Peter answered:
'You are the Christ. The Son of the Living God.'
(Mark 8:29)

Who Do You Say That Jesus Is?

Dear Friends,

One of the greatest battlefronts of our day is, and will increasingly be, the battle over the answer to the following question, first asked by Jesus Christ about Himself:

'Who do you say that I am?'

That question has been ringing through the ages. It is the most important question ever asked, and the temporal welfare of families and of nations and of cultures, not to mention the eternal destiny of millions, depends upon the answer.

Why do I say that this question, and its answer, forms a 'battlefront' in our day? The answer is simply that the question (remember, posed by Jesus Himself), demands an answer that society today will not tolerate. The answer says something exclusive about Truth. Society makes no room today for the only answer which fits the question:

Simon Peter answered:
'You are the Christ. The Son of the Living God.'

Our culture today is asking that you take your beliefs indoors. They don't mind too much if you have some sort of 'private belief'. But Jesus just won't go indoors. He is ever-controversial: 'Do not think I came to bring peace [at the price of Truth]...' The claims of Christ are not boundlessly 'tolerant'. They are at the same time the most *inclusive* claims of all: 'come unto Me *all*...', and the most *exclusive*: 'If you do not believe in Me, you will die in your sins...'

The temptation for the faithful Christian Church in our day will be 1: to 'go private' with its faith, or 2: perhaps even worse, to accommodate a culture which insists that there are 'many ways to God', and that Jesus is just one, maybe even the best, of the many. Either will amount to a giving up of the battle precisely where it is most fiercely raging: over the most important question 'Who is Jesus?' People will not bother a church that waves the white flag of surrender over the issue of who Jesus is. They will even applaud it. Such a church holds no threat. It fits in perfectly to a world that loves a blunt-edged belief. But surrender at this point amounts to apostasy. It means going back on Jesus. It means being unfaithful not only to him, but to our generation that *needs* Him.

As followers of Jesus we offer, under divine directive, the following to the world: Life or Death. Jesus did not come to make bad men better, but, rather, He came to make dead men live. The sad history of our fallen race is strewn with the theories of teachers, good men and bad, who have offered advice and techniques on how to improve ourselves. Christianity offers nothing of the sort. It is an ultimatum and a invitation to men dead in their sins to come to Christ for Life. We are inclusive in that we stand shoulder to shoulder with our fellow sinful humans, freely offering Christ to all. We are exclusive in that it is Jesus Christ that we are offering and none other.

We dare not surrender ground on the issue of Jesus Christ.
   He alone is Lord.
      He alone is Truth.
         He alone is Saviour.
            He alone is the hope of the world.

   He alone emptied Himself of Heaven's bounty to bring salvation to the Rebel Planet.
      He alone dwelt with sinful humanity in sinlessness.
         He alone bled, died, rose again, and ascended in Glory.
            He alone, in the mystery of Triune God, is Life Itself.

   He is not *an* option… not even the *best* option.

      He is the *only* option.
'Who do you say that Jesus is?' This is the question that the Church *must* relentlessly ask the world.

There is no more important question asked, and no more important answer given.

Lets fight the right Battles!

Yours,

John Gillespie.

Notes...

Week 41

Salvation is found in no-one else, for there is no other name under heaven given to men by which we must be saved.
The Apostle Peter (Acts 4:12)

'Yoko and Me' Is Not Reality

Dear Church Family,

Never confuse *Certainty* with *Arrogance*. They are not the same thing. They are not even remotely related to each other, springing from different roots and bearing different fruits.

Arrogance is not becoming to the Christian. No-one likes it when they see it. The Bible does not encourage us to be arrogant, and Jesus does not want it as a part of His disciples' character. Certainty is encouraged in the Bible. Jesus wants us to be certain regarding what we believe to be true and what we believe to be false. For example, Luke tells us that he wrote his gospel 'so that [we] may know the certainty of the things [we] have been taught' (Luke 1:4).

Read the statement by the Apostle Peter at the top of this letter again. It is a statement that expresses *certainty* but not *arrogance*. The statement is not about himself. It is about someone else: Jesus Christ. Arrogance is when we are affirming something about *ourselves* that somehow puts us out of the rank and file of those around us. For instance, an arrogant 'Christian' statement would be:

> 'I have had an experience that has made me a better person.
> If you don't have the same experience as I have had then
> you will go to Hell.'

Do you see the arrogance of the above statement? The person may even be talking about the experience of the forgiveness of sins, but the problem is that the statement is about *himself*. He no longer stands shoulder to shoulder with the rest of humanity. His confidence is located precisely where it should not be: in his own experience.

Contrast Peter's statement. It is not about *himself*, but about *Jesus Christ*. It is full of certainty, but free from arrogance. It is a statement of fact about Christ, whom he is confidently presenting to his hearers. Sure, it lands him, and the whole Church, in trouble, but the charge against him is not arrogance, but inciting insurrection, and blasphemy, with which he sits comfortably (see verses 19,20).

The entire New Testament witness is built upon such confidence, and is free from arrogance. Paul could say to the men of the Areopagus in Athens (the first century equivalent to the Oprah Winfrey Show), 'What you worship as something unknown I am going to proclaim to you' (Acts 17:23). John could write: 'We proclaim to you what we have seen and heard, that you might have fellowship with us' (1 John 1:3). The inspired writers were *un*sure of themselves, but certain of their subject. This is humility, not arrogance. They presented the Gospel as a fact of history, which they and all others were commanded to believe in, not as an experience that they had had which placed them a cut above others.

Now, our world has placed everything back to front, and we Christians have caught the bug. We are now 'sure of ourselves', but not sure about anything else. 'It seems to me...' has become the creed of the age that no one dare argue against. 'My experience' has become sacred truth that no one dare challenge. Truth is now placed precisely where the New Testament never places it, in the very place where arrogance breeds and festers: in the *self*. In keeping with this mix-up, being *sure* about something outside of yourself, like the Gospel, is now considered the very height of arrogance! So, when John Lennon, in his song 'God', boldly sings that he does not believe in God, but just in 'Yoko and Me, and *that's* reality', we fail to see the arrogance of such a claim, and applaud him (albeit posthumously) for his 'honesty and openness'.

The Christian is not called to present *himself* to the world as 'Exhibit A' of what it means to be an amazing person. We are called to present Jesus Christ. We are called to offer a fact of history, of which we are confident, to our generation and plead with them to believe in Him. This is not arrogance, not at all. But our upside-down world may well mis-read it as such. Being confident in the Gospel means that I still recognise my Hindu, Muslim, Atheist or Pagan neighbour as being no different in essence from me. They are *people*, made in God's Image, who, like myself, have a desperate need to be reconciled to God through the One Name that has the power to reconcile.

The New Testament presents Jesus Christ to the world and invites, yes, even commands, faith in Him. Its persuasion is with words, not swords. Its confidence and certainty is in Him, not those who believe in Him.

I leave you with the Bible verse that is the motto of Tessa's and my marriage:

'For we preach not ourselves, but Jesus Christ as Lord.'
(2 Corinthians 4:5)

Yours,

John Gillespie.

Notes:~

*For He has rescued us from the dominion of darkness, and
brought us into the kingdom of the Son He loves, in whom we
have redemption, the forgiveness of sins.
(Colossians 1:13,14)*

'The Mean Altar Of My Heart'

Dear Rescued Ones,

The above truth *ought* to create in us a thankfulness; a gratitude of
life-transforming, sin-severing, mission-motivating magnitude.
When a rescued soul ponders just what it means to be 'rescued
from the dominion of darkness' and 'brought into the kingdom' of
God the Father's beloved Son, there *should* be a resultant and
ongoing transformation of profound proportions in that life. When
the truths spelled out above begin to impact not just individuals,
but a company of believers (a Church), the result can penetrate
even into the dark society surrounding.

Yet I am continually baffled and troubled by the *lack* of impact that
the wonderful Gospel seems to be having... not upon the
*un*believing world, but upon we who profess to be those whom
Christ has rescued and delivered. In fact, I am quite certain that it
is presumptuous of us to expect the Gospel to have a transforming
effect upon the surrounding culture when it is having so little
effect upon *us*.

I sometimes feel as though we respond to the wonders of God's
Grace with a semi-bored yawn... roughly with the same level of
interest that we would have if watching old re-runs of *Dad's Army*
for the umpteenth time.

Far from being a bit bored by it all, our 'rescue from the dominion
of darkness' and deliverance 'into the kingdom' of Jesus should be
so fresh, so recent in our lives' memories, as to at times render us
breathless with joy and awe-struck with amazement that a Holy
God would have had such mercy on such creatures of dust. An
observant Heaven is, and forever shall be, erupting in exuberant
praise to the King of Heaven and the Lamb, who devised and
perfectly executed this, the most daring and costly recovery
mission in all of history.

But how can we move from a place of semi-boredom to rapt awe?
How can we rightly honour and worship God for such a great

salvation? How can the wonders of the Gospel have a true and proper impact upon *us*, that we in turn may have an impact on *others*? Allow me to offer a few helps to personal revival, which I have been given grace to employ in my life:

1. Take time often (daily, even many times a day) to ponder the true value of your soul, which sin and Satan were eternally ruining before Jesus rescued you by His blood. Ask God to open up your heart in grateful praise that you, of all creatures, have been made the special object of God's rescuing, delivering grace (Ephesians 2:4,5). Think about the fact that your soul is of more value than the entire world. Consider Jesus' warnings that to gain the whole world at the expense of your soul is to lose everything (Matthew 16:26). Earnestly ask the Lord to help you understand the worth of your eternal soul.

2. Dwell upon the immeasurable value of the Blood of Jesus Christ, which alone has purchased your redemption from sin, Satan, and death (1 Peter 1:18,19). Again, ask your Heavenly Father to give you a deep revelation of the preciousness of His Son. Don't settle for a glibness about Christ and His Gospel. Insist to your own soul and to your Heavenly Father that you *must* have a heart that truly appreciates the Blood that rescued you or you will be cold, worldly, and of little use to God's Kingdom.

3. Never allow yourself to forget that, even though a true saint is saved and safe with Jesus forever, there are many warnings in the Bible of a counterfeit Christianity, there have been many false followers in history, and that therefore the Word of God admonishes all true believers to regularly examine themselves (2 Corinthians 13:5), that faith in Christ is a precious gift (2 Peter 1:1), and that true saving faith is proven only by holy living and diligent perseverance (Hebrews 12:1-3;14).

Beloved, I have to *actively seek* a Christ-valuing, world-denying heart every day. It does not come to me automatically (the only thing that comes to me automatically is sin). If I leave off seeking a warm heart for a day, I get a cold heart. If I do not ask God for grace to see Him as my Joy and Satisfaction, in no time at all I'll get worldly and lose my Christ-centred contentment.

I'M NOT IN HEAVEN YET!... And neither are you...

All the great saints of History (of which I am not one) have borne testimony of their continual need to seek a warm, grateful, rightly praising heart. You and I can expect nothing

different. I'll leave us with a prayer/hymn of Charles Wesley. May
we make his words our hearts' own:

> O for a heart to praise my God!
> A heart from sin set free.
> A heart which always feels Thy Blood,
> Freely spilled for me!
>
> O Thou Who camest from Above,
> Thy pure celestial fire to impart.
> Kindle a flame of sacred love,
> On the mean altar of my heart.

May the Lord Jesus richly reward our seeking of Him.

Yours,

John Gillespie.

Notes:~

*You are the salt of the earth. But if the salt loses its saltiness,
how can it be made salty again?
It is no longer good for anything, except to be thrown out and
trampled by men.*
— Jesus Christ (the Lord and Creator of the Universe) —

The Real Value Of Salt

Dear Church,

Salt is unmistakable. You always know when it is present; you can
always tell when it is absent.

My father tells a story from his war years about salt. He was stuck
on a troop ship along with hundreds of others off the coast of
France for a period of days with very little to eat. When the
battle situation cleared up, the Army, feeling somewhat beholden
to the men on the ship, sent in a consignment of steak. There was
not enough to go around so the cook, in his wisdom, made beef
stew for the entire ship. Problem: there was not a grain of salt
with which to flavour the stew. Hungry as they were, my father to
this day recalls the unpalatable blandness of that much-needed
meal. He actually wrote my mother a letter back in the States:
'Marty! Send me a box of salt.' She did and he carried that box
of salt across Europe with him for the rest of the War.

Did you know that?...

We get the word *salary* from the word salt. People used to be
paid in salt for their labours.

Cultures would trade gold for salt.

Trade routes were established for the sake of the salt trade.

Wars have been fought over salt.

Cities have been built where salt was plentiful (the Austrian city
of Salzburg is named after salt, literally meaning 'city of salt'.
The city of Buffalo New York is named for a trail that wild
buffaloes forged over the centuries travelling to a salt spring).

Our very cells depend upon the presence of salt. They would die
without it.

Salt has long been used as a preservative, and as a medical curative.

When the Lord of the Universe tells His Redeemed People that we are the salt of the earth, He is saying something most profound about us. Let me sum it up this way:

Salt's *Value*... Our *Value*...
Salt's *Purpose*... Our *Purpose*...
Salt's *Effectiveness*... Our *Effectiveness*...

....is dependent ultimately upon its... our... *Uniqueness*.

Salt is unique in what it is and in what it does. It is unmistakable in its presence and in its influence. There is simply nothing else like it. Salt is *powerful* because it is *different*. We do not want it to be like sugar. We are not interested in it tasting like pepper. We want it to be like... SALT.

Now, there really is only one way for salt to 'lose its saltiness', and that is for it to be adulterated, that is, mixed and diluted by that which is not salt. When salt becomes dirty and diluted, it 'loses its saltiness'. The analogy for us is too obvious to miss:

When we become like the world, we cease to be of influence to the world.
When we try to be trendy we become trivial.
When we try to be 'cool' we end up being clueless.
When we make it our goal to 'be relevant' we end up becoming irrelevant.

We can only make a difference by being different

I do not mean
    Weird,
        Or Prudish,
            Or Isolated,
                Or Wacky

But I do mean
    Heaven-Focused,
        And Jesus-Loving,
           And Sin-Hating,
               And Neighbour-Serving,
               And Self-Denying,
                 And Truth-Embracing

There is nothing more pathetic than when the Church tries to 'be attractive' to the world by being like the world. Unsalty salt! The Bible says it, and history proves it, that when Christians live radically Christ-Centred lives, *they impact their cultures for God and for good*. When Christians try to 'be cool', culture sees right through them and rightly writes them off as irrelevant.

We are called to be Voices, not echoes; Salt, not sugar.

Now, being salt does not necessarily imply swimming the Amazon to reach a tribe or being burned at the stake (although it might...). It can be just as impacting though seemingly far more hum-drum. Dr Michael Horton tells a story, which he claims to be true, about Martin Luther:

Luther was counseling a newly converted Christian man:
'What should I now do to serve Christ? How can I make a difference? Should I become a minister or a missionary?'
[in other words:
'How can I be *salt* in my world?']
'What do you do for a living?' Luther asked.
'I am a cobbler,' replied the newborn man.
Luther answered: 'Then make a good shoe and sell it at fair price.':
SALT!

Dare to be different.

Yours for Him,

John Gillespie.

Notes:~

Week 44

...but David encouraged himself in the LORD his God.
(1 Samuel 30:6)

An Audience Of One

Dear Brothers and Sisters,

I want to speak to you about becoming preachers; Gospel preachers. And I want to encourage you to develop the habit of preaching every day. I want to convince you of the value of preaching every day to a very select audience: yourself.

You heard me right.

I want to encourage you to preach the Gospel to yourself every day. What I mean is this:

Deliberately take time every day to remind yourself of what Christ has done for you in offering Himself as a substitute for your sins (Galatians 2:20)...

Tell your unworthy soul of Christ's love for it in daily offering you His grace and mercy (Lamentations 3:22)

Remind yourself of the eternal certainty of God's covenant of saving love purchased at the cost of His Son's blood (Hebrews 13:20

Declare to yourself the wonders of Christ's perfect righteousness, which has been credited to your account solely because of God's grace (1 Corinthians 1:30)

Take hold of your spirit and make it listen while you speak to it of the glories of Heaven, the horrors of Hell, and the brevity of life (Psalm 19:14)

Take yourself to task over your worldliness, pettiness, selfishness, laziness, and foolishness. Command yourself to repent and come humbly to Christ again (Romans 6:17,18)

Exhort yourself in regards to the needs of the world around you to hear of Christ, and of the treasure you have to share in the Gospel (Romans 1:14,15)

Stir yourself up to worship God for His unfailing kindness to you, an unworthy, flawed, and oft-failing follower (Psalm 103:1)

Tell your tongue that it has been created to praise God and bless others and that to complain and criticise in the face of all God's goodness is wickedness itself (James 3:9-12)

Proclaim to yourself the victory that you have in Christ. You do not have to be a victim this day, because Christ is in you. Tell yourself that it is a sin to feel sorry for yourself (Romans 7:24-25)

Remind your body that it has a soul. Chide it for its vanity and challenge it toward humility and modesty (Romans 12:1)

Tell your emotions that they have no right to expect others to perfectly meet their needs, and no need for others to do so because Christ is your All-Sufficient One
(2 Timothy 4:16)

Reprove your appetites for their resistance to Christ's Lordship and for their constant complaining. Tell them that they will never be lord, because Jesus is (1 Corinthians 10:31)

Instruct your will that it is now subject to your New Nature, which has been redeemed by Jesus and is being renewed in His Image. It can no longer do anything it pleases, but must make choices that honour God (Romans 6:11)

Speak tenderly to your dying frame of the wonders of God's grace, of the power of Christ's resurrection, of the certainty of your future resurrection in glory (1 Corinthians 15:51-54)

Insist to your wants that they cannot always get their way, and that they dare not pout and pull a face because Jesus Christ, your generous Saviour, really is Enough (Philippians 4:19)

Encourage your weary soul with the truth that your accusing enemy, Satan, no longer has any case against you because Christ has triumphed over him for you (Romans 8:37)

Tell your heart to be deeply thankful that it does not have to rely upon people giving you kindness, acceptance and significance, because Jesus already has. Whatever good people bring your way is an unexpected bonus (Psalm 116:7)

Command yourself to forgive others for their failings, refusing self-pity and bitterness, because Jesus Christ has been so rich in mercy and kindness to your undeserving self (Colossians 3:13)

Bring your entire being before your Great God of Grace and thankfully worship Him for all that He is, has been, and promises to be for you through Jesus Christ (Psalm 103:1,2)

Now such preaching, believe me, will be life transforming. It will orient your life rightly. It will deliver you from meaninglessness, irritability, and wasting your days. It will refresh you. It will break the axis-powers of the World, the Flesh, and the Devil, which ever aim to hold you in their death-grip. It will set you on the road to freedom and usefulness. It will deliver you from being tossed about, a hapless victim of life's wind and waves, and put you, in Christ, at the helm of your destiny.

Believer, as I have said so many times before, and will say yet again and again, we become what we want to be in the Christian life. We get out of this what we put into it. You can lay on the sofa and watch Homer eat another donut, or you can get in the Word, get on your knees, get before God's face, and grow... up... and onwards... to maturity in Christ.

You are called to preach... at least, and first, to yourself... every day.

May the Lord Jesus Bless and Anoint your Sermons!

Yours,

John Gillespie.

Notes:~

Week 45

Father, I want those You have given Me to be with Me
where I am, that they may behold My Glory.
(John 17:24)

Do We Dare To Dream?

Dear Family in Christ,

I want to talk to us about dreaming. I mean Big Dreaming. I want to encourage us to be dreamers... Big Dreamers.

Most of us have quit dreaming... too many disappointments. Or, if we are still daring to dream, our dreams have become too small:

> A new car...

> That house we always wanted...

> England winning the World Cup...

> Inheriting a load of money...

The problem with the above dreams is that they are essentially *pagan*. There is no smell of Eternity on them. Anyone can have them, and, to one degree or another, theoretically, almost anyone can see them realised.

I want us to have a Big Dream that captures all lesser dreams and makes them subservient. I long for us to have a Dream that *this life cannot finally satisfy*... a Dream that *demands*...

Eternity.

Now in order to be captured by an Eternity-demanding Dream, in order to be given over to a Dream that requires more than this life has to offer, we need to get a hold of the amazing fact that the LORD of Eternity actually has a Dream for us. Did you know that? Our Dream must spring from His.

Here is Jesus Christ's Dream for us:

> 'Father, I want those You have given Me to be with Me
> where I am, that they may behold My Glory.
> (John 17:24)

Jesus leaves us in no doubt as to His Dream for us. He wants us 1: with Him where He is and 2: beholding His Glory. Notice a couple of things about His Dream for us:

First: It *Demands* Eternity. This life is not long enough for His Dream. This present age cannot finally fulfil the Lord Jesus' heart's desire for His People. I get this from the phrase: 'to be with Me where I am'.

Second: It *Offers* something no lesser dream is capable of offering: participating in the very Glory of Jesus Christ. I get this from the phrase: 'behold my Glory'. The word 'behold' is a fantastic word! It means to look intently or to discern, and implies an ongoing *experience* of the Lord Jesus in His Reality and Majesty.

Jesus' Dream for us involves being together (a redeemed Throng from every tribe and tongue and nation!) in a glorified Heaven, inhabiting glorified bodies that are capable of understanding, participating in, and experiencing HIM... increasingly and forever. In His Dream we all become what He Created and Redeemed us to be. His Dream demands that there be a Heaven, and requires the death of our fallen bodies.

Now, should not *our* Dream spring forth from *His*? Should we not flatly refuse merely earth-bound dreams and urge our souls toward a Heavenly Dream? How can a new car match being with Jesus Christ 'in whom [is] hidden all the treasures of wisdom and knowledge' (Colossians 2:3)? How can the mere passing pleasures of an affair, or a satellite dish purchased at the expense of giving to Dream-fulfilling missions, compete with the God who will 'fill us with Joy in His presence' and with 'eternal pleasures at His right hand (Psalm 16:11)?

Let me cut right to the point: God's Dream for us may be bigger than we are imagining. Chances are we are dreaming pagan dreams... all about this life, the trophies and toys we can accumulate. We live as though we had no souls. We hear Jesus' words: 'No one can serve two masters'; 'What shall it profit a man if he gains the whole world yet forfeits his soul?'; 'Do not lay up treasures on earth... lay up treasures in Heaven...'; but we do not really allow His warnings and encouragements to transform our dreams into His Dream and propel us Heaven-ward.

Our Dream dare not be less than being with our Lord Jesus, engaging increasingly with Him and His Redeemed People in a renewed Creation, becoming all that we were created and redeemed to be, and all for His Glory.

Such a Dream is embraced by Jesus' Dream for us. And get this: such a Dream will wean us from worldliness and motivate us to mission. Our priorities will fall in line with, and serve, such Dream. Life will take on an Eternal significance that lesser dreams simply cannot offer. Sin will lose its power over us in the light of such a Dream. There will be the fragrance of Eternity upon us. Others, those who have quit dreaming, or who know only little dreams, will become Dreamers with us.

Take hold of your soul and give it a shake. Wake it from its slumber and point it Heaven-ward. Pray this prayer with me:

> 'Lord Jesus, I bless You for having a Glorious Dream for Us!
> Lord! Forgive us for and deliver us from our little pagan dreams.
> Give us grace to Dream Your Dream, that together
> our lives may have Eternal Significance.
> To Your Glory and the Joy of all Peoples, Amen.'

Yours,

John Gillespie.

Notes:~

Week 46

*While Jesus was in Bethany in the home of a man known
as Simon the Leper, a woman came with an alabaster jar
of very expensive perfume, which she poured on His head
as He was reclining at the table.*

*When the disciples saw this, they were indignant.
'Why this waste?' they asked.
'This perfume could have been sold at a high price
and the money given to the poor.'
(Matthew 26:6-8)*

The Most Beautiful Act Of Worship

Dear Saints,

Contemplate the above scene with me. It is rich with meaning for
those of us who dare to call ourselves disciples of Jesus Christ.
Imagine yourself for a moment as Simon, the Leper whom Christ
had healed. In gratitude you are happy to have a dinner party for
Jesus Christ! Everything *must* be perfect as you make preparations
for this most important of evenings: the food, the entertainment,
the music, the table carefully set...

As Jesus and the other guests arrive, you, in keeping with social
custom of the day, offer each a drop of perfume for their tired
feet (don't try that today!). Jesus and the others receive it with
thanks and come to recline at your table.

You're nervous...
Expectant...
Excited...

Then, suddenly, unexpectedly, unconventionally, your party is...
crashed...

(Now, switch places and imagine yourself as this gate-crashing
woman.)

You know the custom, women are to stay outside of the dining
room at a formal party... but this is your chance! You have heard
about a prostitute who poured perfume on Jesus' feet in the early
days of His ministry, wiping them with her hair (Luke 7:36ff).
'Wow,' you've thought, 'If ever I have the chance to bless Him in
such a manner, I am going for it.'

Your heart is beating a mile a minute as you approach the house. Past the porch and through the opened door, beyond the foyer and courageously, unbelievably, into the presence of the dining men.

> Jaws drop...
>> Eating stops...
>>> Chatter ceases...

And then... GASPS of shock and disgust as (according to Mark's Gospel), you *break* a vial of *most expensive* perfume and proceed to pour *the entire thing* upon the head of your beloved Jesus.

While Simon and the others are choking on their dinner, Jesus Christ is smiling deeply.

You have broken convention... not a drop on the feet, but a whole bottle on the head.

> You have done what you can
>> While you can
>>> With what you have to give

The others, *even the disciples*, call this extravagance 'Waste'. But you know that this is...

WORSHIP

Jesus knows it too.

This is worship in the deepest and truest sense, perhaps the best example of worship in the whole of sacred Scripture. It goes beyond what is culturally acceptable and is a true expression of a redeemed heart toward a heart's Redeemer. It regards not the opinions of lukewarm on-lookers. It listens not to the rebukes of the culturally religious. It beholds only Christ, its object, and is blessed because *He* is blessed: 'She has done a beautiful thing to me' (v.10).

Now, no more imagination: Be yourself now. Let's *learn* from this remarkable scene and *apply* it to our lives today.

1. The worshipping life that blesses Jesus Christ may be *misunderstood* by others.

2. The worshipping life that blesses Jesus Christ may *shatter* cultural boundaries.

3. The worshipping life that blesses Jesus Christ *gives* what it can, when it can.

4. The worshipping life that blesses Jesus Christ is *extravagant*, not calculating.

5. The worshipping life that blesses Jesus Christ *becomes* an unstoppable fragrance.

6. The worshipping life that blesses Jesus Christ will leave a *lasting legacy* of faith.

The Holy Spirit did not feel it worthwhile to tell us what Simon made for dinner, what others wore, what music was being played. Whatever impresses men often means little to God. What the Holy Spirit wanted to be sure would be remembered was this beautiful act of worship.

Sometimes the normal just won't do.

May our lives learn from this woman. May our hearts long to bless our Redeemer, going beyond the normal, to the extravagant. May we not be afraid to 'waste' ourselves on Christ, knowing that in so doing, our very existence will become a fragrance to all, a witness to our culture that there is a Saviour whose name is Jesus Christ.

Yours, and Willing to be Wasted for His Name's Sake,

John Gillespie.

Notes:~

*I eagerly expect and hope that I will in no way be ashamed,
but will have sufficient courage so that now as always Christ
will be exalted in my body, whether by life or by death.
(Philippians 1:20)*

Treasuring Christ More Than Life

Dear Sisters and Brothers,

I had the great pastoral privilege this past week of performing the
funeral service for a departed follower of Our Lord Jesus. Her
passing, from cancer, has led me to consider the question, 'How
can it *ever* be *more* glorifying to God for one of His children to
suffer and die rather than to be miraculously healed?

I want to address this question for us this week. It is a question
that lingers in the background almost all of the time, and
sometimes brazenly presents itself in the foreground of our lives
and fellowships. It is a question that deserves consideration and
which, I believe, is not impossible to answer.

Now, let me first assure you all that I believe that the Lord Jesus
heals today in answer to believing prayer. It is a great privilege and
joy to pray for the sick. We embrace this ministry with all
earnestness and faith. But simple honesty leads us to admit that
the Lord does not always answer believing prayer in the way we
hope. Precious saints get sick and die of the same diseases that
unbelievers get sick and die of. So, read the question again,
because it is carefully worded:

'How can it *ever* be *more* glorifying to God for one of His children
to suffer and die rather than to be miraculously healed?'

If God truly wills 'all things' to work for 'our good', and if He
really is purposing that He be glorified in all the earth, then
certainly a miraculous deliverance must beat painful suffering and
death every time... Right?

To press the seemingly obvious point a bit further; how can the
Apostle make a statement like the one at the top of this page: 'I
eagerly expect... that... Christ will be exalted [glorified] in my
body [my present physical existence] whether by life or *by death*'?

Or, how can the Psalmist say: '*Precious* in the sight of the Lord is the death of His saints' (Psalm 116:15), or: 'Because Your love is *better* than life, my lips will glorify You' (Psalm 63:3)?

Okay, stick with me now. God can be *more* greatly glorified in a dying believer, and his believing loved ones who minister to him and mourn his loss, **because a true treasuring of Christ above all things is displayed only when death is faced**. A dying believer who says: 'To depart and be with Christ is *better* by far,' displays a valuing of Christ that astounds and confounds the world. A sick saint who says: 'Because your love is *better* than life, my lips will glorify you,' is exalting Christ above life itself. The watching world knows no such power, and has no answer for it. It is the ultimate witness to Christ.

Now, of course Christ is magnified in a physical healing, as often are doctors. But agree with me: everybody likes getting better! Wanting to get better is not unique to Christians! Non-believers like that too! Wanting to get better affirms our love for our families, our homes, our present world. Christians and non-Christians alike value these visible things. That is okay, and understandable. It is *natural*. Treasuring Christ more than life is **super***natural*!

Let me write that again:

        Treasuring Christ more than life is **super***natural*!

It is the result of Grace working deep in the soul. Treasuring Christ more than life ultimately REQUIRES death, not healing. Dying well, as an act of worship, and facing the death of those whom we love well, is the sole reserve of Heaven-minded Christians.

This is why saints of old, like John Wesley (who prayed for the sick and saw physical healings), studied 'how to die well'. He loved a book written by a saintly Jeremy Taylor called *Rules for Holy Living and Dying*. At the Methodist Annual Conference he asked his preachers to report 'triumphant deaths'. Why? Because such deaths speak unspeakable words of devotion to Jesus Christ, and confidence in His Saving Work. 'Triumphant deaths' glorify Christ *even more than* 'triumphant healings' because those who are involved in the triumph have no treasure, no hope, no joy other than Christ, *and this becomes clear to all around them*. This treasuring of Christ does not make everything easy, but it does support the soul when all other supports have shattered.

Mercy's full power is displayed when the believer has nothing left besides Jesus *and worships Him as enough*!

I hope that I have helped you to see, for the good of your souls, how God is *even more* magnified in the suffering and death of His precious child of grace than in their healing. I leave you with the stanza of an ancient Methodist hymn:

> Fixed on this ground will I remain,
> Though my heart fail, and flesh decay;
> This anchor shall my soul sustain,
> When earth's foundations melt away;
> Mercy's full power I then shall prove,
> Loved with an everlasting love.
> *J A Rothe (1688-1758)*
> *tr. John Wesley (1702-1791)*

Yours,

John Gillespie.

Notes:~

Week 48

For the Joy of the Lord is Your Strength.
(Nehemiah 8:10)

God Has Never Been Depressed!

Dear Church Family,

I want to let you in on my personal battle for Joy, and share with you one of my most precious discoveries. I am sure that I am not the only one who has found Joy to be often elusive, perhaps not the only one who has battled often with melancholy of spirit.

Of two things we can be certain:

      1: Jesus wants us Joyful
      2: Satan does not

I could marshal countless Scriptures to prove the above two truths but one will be sufficient, for it falls from the lips of the Lord Jesus Himself:

'The thief [you know who that is] comes to
steal and kill and destroy.
I have come that they [that's us!] might have life and have
it to the full.'
(John 10:10)

Now, true Joy goes deeper than happiness, and is not dependent upon shallow earthly sources. The verse at the top of this letter takes us right to the source of true Joy. The discovery of this source has become to me personally *my* source of Joy. The verse sources Joy in the very nature of God, and then makes the life-transforming link between *His* Joy and *our* well-being. Walk with me up the mount of God and refresh your soul with me in this Eternal Source of all Joy; God Himself.

Okay, here is the key to my discovery: God, the Eternal Triune Father, Son, and Holy Spirit **is in His very nature a Community of Joy.** He likes being God. **He has never been depressed.** Within the relationship that is the Trinity there has never been an argument. Go to the spiritual heart of the Universe and there you will find our Triune God, *full of Joy.*

Now, just take some time and *think* about this. Let it wash over your Joy-parched soul. Let the Joy of the Lord slake *your* thirst for deep, deep Fullness. Our Joy is sourced in the very nature of God. It is not sourced, it *dare not be sourced,* in anything less than the very way that God actually *is*.

Allow a human analogy:

As the head of my family, my mood sets the mood of the entire household. I am prone to moodiness (God is not). If I am in a sad mood, the kids are sad, my wife is affected, the entire household feels it. If I am glad, my home is glad. If my emotions are under peaceful control, my house is generally at peace. It is as simple and profound as that.

Now, our God is Joyful within Himself. *His* Joy should affect *His* family, right down to you and me. If God is not freaking out, then I don't need to be either. *His* mood needs to be the source, the determiner, of *my* mood.
This truth needs to be meditated upon, chewed upon. We have become too emotionally fragile. We are not resourcing ourselves in our changeless God, but in transient things. For years I have been at the mercy of my moods, a victim of the winds that blow about me (and blow me about). God has really been challenging me of late to deal with this... impressing upon my heart that it is actually a sign of spiritual immaturity to allow myself to be affected so by everything but Himself. To put it bluntly, if He is Joyful, I should be Joyful. It just may be a sinful, unbelieving heart that allows me to wallow in joyless melancholy when I am called to believe for, and battle for, Joy.

So, I have begun to battle instead of wallow, strengthening my spirit with Scripture Truths. Boy! Do I have a long way to go, but having *seen* truth that Joy resides at the relational centre of our Triune God, and that His Joy is available for my strengthening, a revolution has begun in my soul.

I hope that this is speaking to some hearts which, like mine, to one degree or another, have known unexplainable dark days. But just in case you need yet a bit more encouragement to believe that the Lord would like *His* Joy to be in *You*, let me leave you with the very words of our Lord Jesus. Take them, believe them, refuse to accept any less than what He is offering you:

'As the Father has loved me, so have I loved you...
I have told you this so that my Joy may be in you,
and that your Joy may be complete.'
(John 15:9,11)

May the Joy that exists in the very nature of our God become for us
an inexhaustible fount of Fullness.

Grace and Peace,

John Gillespie.

Notes:~

Week 49

...our old self was crucified with Him...
(Romans 6:6)

Let's Kill The Old Man

Dear Friends,

In 1944 Japanese soldier Lt Hiroo Onoda was sent by his commanding officer to the remote Philippine island of Lubang to conduct guerilla warfare and spy upon his Allied enemies.

He surrendered thirty years later, in 1974. He refused to believe that the war had ended.

As a teenager, I remember seeing the event on the news.

He had spent twenty-nine years fighting a war that had already been decided, battling on even though he had already been defeated. During those years he lived on the run, in hiding, on the lookout. He, and the small troop of soldiers who held out with him (all of whom had died by 1974) had killed more than thirty Filipinos, believing themselves to be still in a state of hostility, convinced that victory would be theirs.

Onoda had had his chances; the Allies leafleted the island from the air telling of their victory and of the end of hostilities. He found the leaflets, but refused to believe that Japan could ever lose the war. Island peoples, aware of his shadowy existence, left newspapers telling of peace where he could find them, but in his growing paranoia, he believed such news to be a hoax or, worse, a trap.

So he went on polishing his rifle, living rough, keeping watch, and killing... all for no purpose.

Finally, in 1974, his aged commanding officer, hearing of his existence, travelled to Lubang, found him, and gave him the now old news... he had been defeated long ago. It was time now to lay down the arms, and face the facts!

Can you imagine how he felt when he discovered the folly of his ways? We need not imagine, we have his words:

'Suddenly a storm raged inside of me...
Everything went black...
I felt like a fool...'

Now, the Onoda misadventure is pregnant with applications, but I want simply to draw out one, and then drive home a point.

I want you to imagine with me that our brave but blundering warrior is a picture of us as individuals... at least of a part of us. I am referring to what theologians call the 'sinful nature' or 'the old man'. Do you know that the 'natural' once-born human being is actually *controlled by* a nature that is at war with God and refuses to give up? As unpalatable as that might sound, it is what the Bible teaches. Hear the Apostle Paul on this:

As for you, you were dead in your transgressions and sins,
in which you used to live when you followed the ways of this world and the ruler of the kingdom of the air, the spirit who is at work in those who are disobedient. All of us lived among them at one time *gratifying the cravings of our sinful nature and following its desires and thoughts*. Like the rest we were by nature objects of wrath... (Ephesians 2:1-3)

Now this sinful nature 'naturally' has dominion over every one of us... even over every baby born on this planet (just watch a crèche for a few minutes). The very guilt and pollution of Adam has been passed on to us so that we now sin by nature and by choice. This is what theologians call the 'Doctrine of Original Sin'. Don't like that? Hear King David on this:

Surely I was sinful at birth,
Sinful from the time my mother conceived me...
(Psalm 51:5)

Now hear some Good News, good for your soul, but bad for your 'sinful nature'. Your 'sinful nature' has been soundly defeated through the death of Jesus Christ on the Cross. A decisive victory has been secured over Satan and sin through the death and resurrection of Jesus Christ. Don't believe me? Well then, believe the Bible:

I [the 'old man'] have been crucified with Christ,
and I [the 'old man'] no longer live, but Christ lives in me...
(Galatians 2:20)

Knowing this, that our old self was crucified with Him,
that the body of sin [the 'old man'] *might be done away with,*
that we should no longer be slaves to sin...
(Romans 6:6)

We have moved Kingdoms, been given new natures, and have been
adopted out of Adam's family (yes, the whole human race is
naturally, literally 'The Adam's Family'), and into Christ's.

Everything is New For the Believer!

But...

...There is a good chance that your sinful nature has not gotten
the message.

And...

...As long as you give 'him' the least bit of encouragement to fight
on, he will. He will creep around, living in the shadowy areas of
your life, hiding here and there, taking any and every opportunity
to inflict damage and havoc, refusing to believe that he will ever
be defeated.

What needs to happen to your 'sinful flesh' is the same thing that
needed to happen to Onoda. Somebody, namely *You*, needs to
inform him, in no uncertain terms, that he has been defeated (at
Calvary), and he has *no chance of winning*. The Bible says so:

Count yourselves dead to sin but alive to God in Christ Jesus...
(Romans 6:11)

Sin shall not be your master, because you are not under the law,
but under grace... (Romans 6:14)

We were therefore buried with Him through baptism into death, in
order that, just as Christ was raised from the dead through the
glory of the Father, we too may live a new life... (Romans 6:4)

If any one is in Christ, he is a New Creation. The old has gone, the
new has come... (2 Corinthians 5:17)

So I say, live by the Spirit, and you will not gratify the desires of
the sinful nature... (Galatians 5:16)

We need to be tough on him, and give him no space for negotiations.

Look, the make-up of a human is very complex, and the fact of a sinful nature does not make it any easier to figure us out. But the bottom line is that the Believer has a *new* nature, and the old nature needs to be told so... as often as necessary, until it gets the message. ('Crucifying the sinful nature' is a Bible way of saying the same thing.) Could it be that a lot of us are living under the influence of an old foe that needs to be confronted with the FACT of Christ's victory, disarmed and marched off in chains? Sin's *penalty* was paid for on Calvary's Cross, and sin's *power* was broken on that very same Cross!

Jesus Christ has come to set us free. Jesus said: 'If the Son sets you free, you shall be free indeed' (John 8:36). Is your 'old man' still 'at large', refusing to believe that he has been defeated on the Cross, holding you in bondage to sin, fear, and defeat? Tell him in no uncertain terms that *he* is finished and that *you* are now a New Creature, in Christ, created to do good works, pleasing to God, with a new heart and a new life, called 'holy' by God Himself, uniquely *His*...

A Victor, and Not a Victim Any more!

Yours,

John Gillespie.

Notes:~

The Word became flesh and made His dwelling among us.
(John 1:14)

An Out Of This World Experience

Dear Grace Family,

In his true book, *Destination Moon*, astronaut James Irwin tells of his encounter with Jesus Christ... on the Moon... you read that right... *On the Moon.*

James Irwin, the last man to walk the surface of our Moon, left Earth's orbit at best a nominal Christian, if one at all. It was while all but weightless on the Lunar surface that the full weight of his sin and the wonders of Jesus Christ began to press upon him.

Irwin, scientist and astronaut, returned to Earth a changed man!

One of his most memorable reflections is found in the quote:

'Man walking on the Moon is not so amazing as God walking on the Earth.'*

Indeed! There is *nothing* so wonderful, so amazing, so significant, as the message we celebrate at Christmas. Charles Wesley, not a scientist but a poet, put it this way:

> 'Our God contracted to a span;
> Incomprehensibly made Man.'

I would suggest to you that the *Incarnation*, that is, God becoming a human being in Jesus Christ, fully God and fully man *at the same time*, is the most profound miracle of all miracles.

Lois Berkhof, a theologian, put it this way:

'Miracle of Miracles, [a] mystery which defies explanation.'

Wayne Grudem (known to many of us through his *Systematic Theology*) puts it this way:

'It is by far the most amazing miracle of the entire Bible — far more amazing than the resurrection and even more amazing than the creation of the universe.'

I want to encourage us to *ponder* the wonder of this miracle of miracles. The Incarnation sets Jesus Christ, the man, apart from the rest of us, *and, at the same time*, makes Jesus Christ, the Eternal Son of God, one of us! The New Testament narratives are economical in their descriptions of God becoming a man. They really don't tell us much. They declare the mystery, but they don't unlock it... for it is beyond our grasp. They leave us to worship like the Wise Men, and, like Mary, to 'treasure up these things and ponder them in [our] heart.' (Luke 2:19)

You can do your soul no better than to consider the endless facets of our Lord and Saviour. Please put aside some time to do just that.

Every blessing,

John Gillespie.

(*I quote this from memory... I have retained the essence of what Irwin said.)

Notes:~

*For I am already being poured out like a drink offering,
and the time has come for my departure.
I have fought the good fight, I have finished the race,
I have kept the faith. Now there is in store for me the crown of
righteousness, which the Lord, the Righteous Judge, will award to
me on that day — and not only to me, but also to all who have
longed for His appearing.*
(The Apostle Paul; 2 Timothy 4:6-8)

How Well Will You Die?

Dear Family,

My suitcase is packed and I am leaving this afternoon for Kansas
City as my mother's death is imminent. I want to briefly reflect
upon her death in order to encourage us in our lives.

The simple, profound lesson from her, and from all believers who
die well is this:

To Die well, One must Live well

Not every one dies well. Not every *believer* dies well. Many die
with bitterness, regrets, sorrows and heartaches. The old-time
Christians lived well so that they could die well. They ran with an
aim of finishing strong. They made their decisions in light of their
end. They thought of more than just the moment. They planned
beyond the weekend... they planned for Eternity.

Like many from her generation, my mother experienced the
Depression (her father's firm went bankrupt), the War (her
husband, my father, was in active duty for two years in Europe),
and then the dangerous affluence of the past forty years. She
earnestly dedicated me to the Lord Jesus at my birth, and then
surrendered me and my family to a call to the other side of the
world nearly a quarter of a century ago. I have seen her for about
one week per year for the last twenty-three years. But she has
prayed earnestly for me, my home, and this church all the way
along. We have been very close, and the miles have not separated
our hearts. She has been the gracious matriarch of our family.

My daughter Bethany telephoned her dying grandmother yesterday.
As my sister held the phone to her ear, Bethany heard her
grandmother say, 'I have had a wonderful life.' Her speech was all
of grace and God's goodness. The preciousness of the Lord Jesus

has been evident in her life for years, but is magnified in her dying days.

Now, friends, this will not happen to us by accident. We need to *apply ourselves* to Godliness. We, naturally, will grow more selfish and irritable as time goes on. Dying to self... daily, and living to Christ... daily, is the only remedy. Otherwise, poor decisions, made with no thought of Forever, will haunt us in our final days. If we will die well, we need to make decisions *today* in the light of *tomorrow*. If we will die well, we need to allow God to do His pruning work in our lives today, shaping us with His masterful hands into the fruitful people He intends for us to be.

My dear mother is bearing much fruit as she dies. Love, joy, peace, patience, kindness, goodness, faithfulness and self-control are plainly evident in her life. The fruit is ripe and the branches are bending low with richness.

Would you not have it to be so with yourself? How do you wish to be remembered? Do you not long to live a life that reflects the beauty of your Saviour to a world which sees so much pain, and the ugliness of sin? Do you not want to be a part of the solution, and not a part of the problem? Then *press into God and His Grace*. Make much of Jesus Christ and His Atoning Blood shed for you. Make the tough decisions *now* to crucify your flesh and pursue holiness of heart and life. Joyfully follow hard after God. Make even your little choices in the light of your last day and Eternity beyond. Study to die well and you will live well. Keep the goal in mind, and the destination in view.

Well, I must go. I will miss you this Christmas time. You are all very precious to me, and I am privileged to be your pastor.

Let's make this life count.... for Eternity's Sake.
Yours,

John Gillespie.

Notes:~

...for tomorrow I will do wondrous things among you.
(Joshua 3:5)

Are You Willing To Consecrate Yourself?

Dear Family in Christ,

Do you ever find yourself reading your Bible when suddenly a verse, one that you have most certainly read many times before, comes to life before you and speaks to you as though you have never even seen it before?

Well, that happened to me this past week while I was having my early morning quiet time. I was sitting in my father's chair at his home in Kansas City reading the Book of Joshua, when the following verse jumped up and grabbed me:

> 'Consecrate yourselves, for tomorrow I will do wondrous things among you.' (Joshua 3:5)

Now, you need to believe me when I tell you that I actually believe that *God* speaks to me (and to all who are ready to listen) through the Bible. My quiet times with God are life and breath to me, because I meet with Him through His Word... He speaks to my heart and into my life situation almost every day.

He spoke to me last week in the verse above, and I am pleased to share with you what He shared with me.

First, let's remember the background:

Israel had been wandering for forty years in the wilderness, God forbidding them to enter the Promised Land due to their sin of unbelief. Moses, their leader through those years of disobedience, was now dead and buried, and Joshua had succeeded him as the leader of God's Israel. It was Joshua who was to lead Israel over the Jordan river to take possession of the Land He had promised
to them.

What plans God had for them! He was to lead them in victory over their enemies and establish them as His prized people, as a testimony to all the world of His grace and power. He was about to fulfil in them the promises He had made centuries before to

154

Abraham. He was about to prove Himself to be their Covenant-Keeping Faithful God in giving them their long-promised inheritance. He was ready to 'do wondrous things' among them.

But God's readiness and willingness led to a call for consecration among God's people. This was what grabbed my heart on that early morning in Kansas City. '*Consecrate yourselves*... for tomorrow I will do wondrous things among you.' To consecrate yourself means...

> To set yourself apart from all that is unholy
>> To repent of any sin that may be found in you
>>> To get serious about God again
>>>> To open your heart up to the Lord in a new way

God was not going to take a half-hearted, worldly people into the Promised Land. Such a people would never stand up to the battles and challenges involved in taking that land for the Lord. More so, a worldly, carnal Israel would make a mess of God's abundant goodness, receiving the blessings, but forgetting the Lord.

An unconsecrated people are unfit both for the battles and the blessings God has in store for them.

Likewise, what was true for ancient Israel is true for me today.

> Does God want to bless me? **YES**
> Does God want to lead me to victory in battle? **YES**
> Does God have great plans for me as His son? **YES**
> Does God have glorious purposes for me to walk into? **YES**

Can God use me as fully as He desires to if I am half-converted, worldly, selfish and essentially no different than the world around me?
NO!

My private life matters. My relationships matter. What I think about matters. How I spend my money matters. What I say matters. My habits and hobbies are important. Every aspect of my life matters and needs to be consecrated... set apart... for God's greater Glory.

Half-heartedness is an offence to our Gracious God and stifles His Glorious Purposes for us.

God's word to Israel so long ago became a word to me for today, for this coming year. Now is the time for me to rid myself of all that is not holy, and to open my heart yet more to the Lord, for His Heart is to do 'wondrous things' in my life and circumstances. God has battles for me to fight... and win, and blessings for me to receive and rejoice in.

Could His word to me be a word for you, and for us as a church in the coming year?

I believe so! God wants and wills 'to do wondrous things among us', but the Key is in our hands: 'Consecrate yourselves'.

Let's not be afraid of Holiness of Heart and Life. Allow me to get 'up close and personal' for just a moment or two:

What will 'consecrating yourself' *look like* in *your* life?
    What choices will you have to make?
        What repentances might you have to make?
            What relationships may need to be mended?
                What shape will 'dying to self' take in your life?

Don't allow yourself to dodge these questions. Your ability to fight and win the battles God has for you, to scale the mountains He has for you, and to inherit the blessings He has for you, depends upon your ardent willingness to 'consecrate yourself' to Him.

But, the challenge cannot rest with me, or with you, as individuals. The challenge from Joshua 3:5 was for Israel *as a people*. God is calling *us*, not just me, not just you, but *US*, as a company of believers, as a body of believers, to 'consecrate ourselves'... as individuals, but as individuals *who belong to* each other. How we each rise to this will have an effect upon the whole. As a church God has battles for *us* to fight and win for the Gospel, and abundant blessings for *us* to inherit.

Consecrating myself is about something bigger than just me, my battles, my blessings. In the end it is about the welfare of the People of God, and the advancement of the cause of Christ on Earth.

Beloved, God wants and wills to 'do wondrous things among us'. May we, each one, and as a whole as we face a New Year, 'Consecrate ourselves' in every way to Him that we may be in the place to fight and win battles and receive and rejoice in blessings.

Yours for the Kingdom,

John Gillespie.

As for me, far be it from me that I should sin against the LORD
by failing to pray for you.
And I will teach you the way that is good and right.
(The prophet Samuel to the People of God, 1 Samuel 12:23)

Notes:~

A Pastor's Prayer At Close Of Day

Heavenly Father, I am humbled by the privilege of praying for Your People, those whom You have purchased at the cost of Your Son's life, those whom You have delivered from wrath, and upon whom You have in Sovereignty set Your love. Lord, as I pray I remember the undeserved miracle which You have worked in them, in bringing them from death to life, from the dominion of darkness to Your Kingdom of Light, from the empty way of life handed down to them, to a new Life of Eternal purpose and glory. Lord, I remember that these are Your people, and Holy Nation, and Royal Family. Lord! I bless You for the miracle that is the Church, Your People, of whom I am called to be a shepherd.

God, Holy God, whose eyes are too pure to look upon evil, I pray, with all my heart, that You will do a deep work in the lives of these, Your People. Father! That they, that we, would increasingly love You above all else. That their affections and desires would be increasingly turned away from the temporary and trivial, and to the Eternal and Meaningful. Cause them to hate sin, Lord, by opening their eyes to see Your Beauty and the Preciousness of your Dear Son. Give me, and my colleagues, grace to show them Yourself, and nothing less, in the Scriptures. Give them hearts for You, Heavenly Father... hearts of flesh and not of stone, hearts that yearn for the Real, hearts that cannot be satisfied with anything less than Your Own Self. Move upon Your People in a new way. Stir hearts and minds to love the things You love, and hate the things You hate. Bring us together to new places of repentance, cleansing, freedom, and joy.

Father, I do not, I *cannot*, pray that we simply have easy, pleasurable lives. I ask for *meaningful* lives. I realize that there is an enemy that will rock us into a sleep of death, if he can. I would want us disturbed, Lord, stirred from slumber, and agitated! Give us a holy defiance to say 'no' to the Siren song that beckons us towards the seemingly easy way. Save us from the death that comes with pursuing personal peace and personal prosperity above all else... Even worse, save us from believing that Your Son is here to serve *our* self-interests. It is a hard prayer, Lord, but bring us all to a place where we can truly say: 'Jesus is my Enough'. Faithful and Good God, even if You have to inflict trial, tribulation, and loss upon us to wean us from this world, and bring us to a new place of treasuring Your Own Self, Lord, this pastor asks You to do it.

Father, I don't know if I can put my heart into words, so I now beg the help of Your Holy Spirit; I pray that You will do two seemingly contrary things in us, Lord: Ruin us, Your people, for the 'ordinary', and, at the very same time cause us to value every ordinary day, and even every ordinary moment. At one and the same time, may those whom I pastor never again be able to be satisfied with things that their neighbours run after, but, strangely, may they find their hearts worshipping You in a good day's work, a warm, tasty meal, and in the embrace and fellowship of one another. Give us that amazing Grace that enables us to lose ourselves, yet gain True Life; to deny ourselves, yet laugh and love. Lord, make us *both* Heavenly and 'Earthy', like Jesus was when He walked upon our planet, looking toward Eternity, but hallowing Time. Make us radical, but not weird, Lord.

And, Lord, I pray that you give these Your People, the pastors they need. I pray for myself and for my colleagues. Lord! Make us faithful men. Cause us at one and the same time to love Your People, but not to fear them. Give them prophets, not politicians, shepherds, not hirelings. Set both Your Terror and Your Love upon us, Lord. May we rather die than fail to teach and preach the Truth to Your People, but may we do it with hearts that brim and break with Your very Heart for them. Make us men of fidelity and constancy. Give us grace to study hard, to preach searching messages, to press Your People for holiness of heart and life, and to equip them to serve the Cause of Christ in our day.

My God, there is so much more in my heart to pray. But weariness and bedtime draws my time to a close. May I just ask, Lord Jesus, that you cause us to stand as one man for the Gospel, joyfully contending together for the fame of Your Name, to the joy of all Peoples. Give us deep love for Yourself, for each other, and for the world for which You have shed Your very own blood. And, Lord, in this brief and uncertain life, grant us the Grace to live each day as though it is our last, for, indeed, it might be. Make us able and ready to embrace death, knowing that in Christ we have found Life, and that to the full.

I pray these things for your Glory and for the Good of those whom I and my colleagues have been graciously called to pastor.

Amen.

A Meditation On Missing Church

Dear Family,

I skipped church last Sunday. Tessa and I found ourselves with a week off in a sleepy little town in Norfolk.

Sunday morning rolled around... and I didn't feel like going to church. So, I did the standard ['what a wonderful guy I am'] husband thing:

> 'You go, sweetheart.'
> 'I really want you to.'
> 'Have a great time.'
> 'I'll have lunch ready when you get back.'

Off went Tessa, on her own...

I learned a lot that morning about myself, the needs of my soul, the value of the Body of Christ and the preciousness of The Lord's Day.

First of all, upon observation, I realise that the entire morning proved to be nothing but an exercise in self-indulgence.

> I made another cup of tea
> I watched a bit of Television (World Athletics Championships)
>
> I took a snooze

Then, as self-indulgence-produced boredom began to set in, I strolled up to the corner shop to get a paper. By now I was blending in perfectly with post-Christian, secular, British paganism. In my shorts and sandals (*with* socks), there was now *nothing* to distinguish me on that bright Sunday morn as a twice-born member of an Eternal Kingdom. I began to feel uneasy inside. As I entered the paper shop, brushing up alongside all others who saw Sunday morning as 'their time', I wanted to say: 'I don't usually do this... I normally join with all the others who worship the Eternal God, the Maker of the Heavens and the Earth...' I vainly hoped as I perused the papers that my comrades in self-indulgence could see something transcendent in me... something of another Kingdom (perhaps the socks?). But it was of no avail... like a chameleon, I had perfectly taken on the hues of the world around me.

By the time Tessa returned from church, my soul was hungry. I wanted, no, *needed*, to know all about her *encounter with the*

Living God via her gathering with the People of God under the Word of God that morning.

> 'Tell me about the Sermon.'
> 'What hymns did you sing?'
> 'Were there any children?'

Upon closer self-inspection, I realised that there was a certain *conceit* in my decision to have a 'Sunday off'. Such a conceit devalued the Body of Christ. I assumed that the sermon would probably not be all that good (in fact, it wasn't very good, but Tessa *worked* at it a bit, *chewed* on it, and thereby received nourishment from it). Ignoring my own admonishments from my own church's pulpit to my own congregation, I reasoned that the music may not be to my liking (as if *my* liking has *anything at all* to do with its value to God). But by the time I had shuffled back from the newsagent's my decision, born of conceit, had served to teach me a lesson in humility.

I *need* the Body of Christ. Wherever I am, and wherever it gathers, I *need* to be present with it. I *need* to put myself *under* the ministry of Word and Sacrament. I *need* to bring my heart and mind and will to worship the Living God. Another Sunday or two like the one I had just spent (wasted), and my soul would be seriously feeling it. There is something very **right**, very **beneficial**, about the **discipline** of 'going to church', whether one feels like it or not. It reminds the soul that it has a God whom it needs and to whom it is accountable. Sunday is a gift from God, precious, given to His Church, His Bride, His Body, to gather and worship and be fed.*

But more, the Body of Christ *needed me* that morning. That little church on the corner in Norfolk is a valiant out-post of God's Kingdom in the midst of Babylon. Each local church, as it gathers, shouts a defiant 'NO' to the Christ-defying culture around it. Families, young people, pensioners (and holiday-makers) who rise and choose to gather with others *because of Jesus* are bearing a profound witness *just by doing so*. They are holding back the flood of secularism. They are being salt and light in the very act of gathering together. They are loving their communities, each other, and their Lord Jesus. I did not help them to do any of that as I yawned my way through 'my' Sunday morning. Perhaps these are some of the reasons why the Bible admonishes us:

> 'Do not forsake meeting together,
> as some are in the habit of doing.'
> (Hebrews 10:25)

161

Well, your pastor learned a lesson. Let us never belittle the value of gathering together on a Sunday Morning to worship the Lord Jesus.

Can't wait for Sunday!

Yours,

John Gillespie.

*There is every indication in the New Testament that the early Church began to meet on Sundays, as their special day of worship, in celebration of the Resurrection. See, for example, Acts 20:7; 1 Corinthians 16:2; Revelation 1:10.

*But if it is preached that Christ has been raised
from the dead, how can some of you say that
there is no resurrection of the dead?
If there is no resurrection of the dead, then not
even Christ has been raised. And if Christ has not
been raised, our preaching is useless and so is your
faith. More than that, we are then found to be false
witnesses about God, for we have testified about God
that He raised Christ from the dead. But He did not
raise Him if in fact the dead are not raised. For if
the dead are not raised, then Christ has not been
raised either. And if Christ has not been raised, your
faith is futile; you are still in your sins. Then those
also who have fallen asleep in Christ are lost.
If only for this life we have hope in Christ, we are to
be pitied more than all men.*

*And as for us, why do we endanger ourselves every
hour? I die every day — I mean that, brothers — just
as surely as I glory over you in Christ Jesus our Lord.
If I fought wild beasts in Ephesus for merely human
reasons, what have I gained? If the dead are not
raised, 'Let us eat and drink, for tomorrow we die.'*
(The Apostle Paul 1 Corinthians 15)

The Greatest Event in the History of the Universe

Dear Friends,

Today I want us to consider the impact of the Apostle Paul's
position on the Resurrection upon how we view the Christian claim
that Jesus Christ is risen from the dead. Notice with me three
things:

1. The Apostle has no time for a sentimental religion that is not
historically true. If we make a claim that Christ has risen when in
fact He has not we are false witnesses (liars!) and our Christianity is
not only futile, it is actually wicked.

2. Proclaiming the Resurrection has been a costly thing for Paul.
The Resurrection has caused him trouble! He proclaims it because it
is true, not because it is popular.

3. If the Resurrection is not true, Paul advises that we choose a life of pleasure-seeking hedonism because, in the end, life is meaningless. There are no other options for Paul. He won't go back to the emptiness of Judaism, and other philosophies and religions lead nowhere.

There is absolutely no room for sentimentality over the Resurrection for the Apostle. He would never say (as I have heard some of us say): 'Well, even if it is not true, I still want to follow Jesus because it feels so nice... the "earthly" benefits are so good.' 'NO!' says Paul to such thinking. This man follows Christ because he is convinced that Jesus Christ is the Risen Lord and therefore the Ultimate Truth and the only answer for the cries of the human heart.

Brothers and Sisters, the Resurrection is an ultimatum from Heaven. 'Easter' may be about bunnies and chocolates, but the Resurrection is about the only hope for a wicked and wayward planet. We dare not tone it down. We dare not default to sentimentalism over it. If it is True, if indeed Jesus Christ is Risen (and I believe that He IS), then this Gospel is worth our all. If we believe it NOT to be true, then walk away from it we must... (but to what?).

These are the only two options. To be 'sentimental' without conviction is not an available option... The stakes are too high.

On Resurrection Sunday let's reverently and joyfully celebrate the Greatest Event in the History of the Universe.

Yours for Him,

John Gillespie.

Notes:~

Other Day Three Editions Books

My And My Bleeding Mouth
by Sue Weller
the painful true story of Gary McCormick

Gary was born in Northern Ireland the year the  Irish Troubles began. And trouble was what he fell into, constantly. Arrested for the first time at the age of twelve Gary climbed the penal ladder adeptly. It wasn't as if he was a hardened criminal; at every twist and turn Gary intended to change his ways, but his personality, and his mouth, worked against him. This book tells about his struggles to change his life, and includes a chapter on his time spent in a monastery, courtesy of the BBC.

Not The Perfect Church
by Sue Weller

This is the story of Grace Community Church.  Its beginnings came as a result of much pain and struggles for pastor John Gillespie and his family and congregation. The book is not always comfortable reading but it does tell what God can do in the face of what seem to be insurmountable problems, and how He can use our imperfections to bring about His perfect will.

Published by
DAY THREE EDITIONS
Maritime Books
Lodge Hill
Liskeard
PL14 4EZ
Tel 01579 343663

If you would like to find out more about our family of churches,
go to:

www.graceccmorval.co.uk
www.torpointcc.org.uk
www.bodmincommunitychurch.com

A selection of John Gillespie's sermons
are available online,
see www.graceccmorval.co.uk
The sermons are also available on CD

Grace Family Bible Week
A holiday with a difference inspired by God!

See www.gfbwmorval.co.uk

For more information contact the church office as follows:

Grace Community Church
Oak Trees
Morval
Looe
Cornwall
PL13 1PR

Church Office telephone 01503 240930
Mon - Fri 09.30 - 12.30

Author's proceeds from this edition
are in support of
Lenny Rogers' New Life Farm, Kosovo